D1142082

A Pocket Book on

Eggs

Appetizing ways with everyones' favourite food

Shirley Gill

Octopus Books

Contents

First published 1984 by
Octopus Books Limited
59 Grosvenor Street
London W1

© 1984 Octopus Books Limited

ISBN 0 7064 2069 1

Produced by Mandarin Publishers Ltd
22a Westlands Road, Quarry Bay,
Hong Kong

Introduction

Eggs are probably the most versatile of all foods. Available all year round and still relatively cheap in comparison with other protein foods, they are a rich source of iron, protein and vitamins, as well as being low in calories.

In cookery, they can be boiled, fried, baked, poached, scrambled, and used for omelettes. Added to other foods, eggs are the magical ingredient in soufflés, cakes, batters and custards. They thicken and enrich soups, sauces and dressings, bind stuffings and croquette mixtures, glaze pies and tea-time scones and clarify consommés and jellies.

You will find here all the basic egg recipes with the different cooking techniques clearly explained, followed by a selection of delicious dishes for every occasion — breakfast, lunch, supper, desserts, entertaining and many more.

Nutritional content

Eggs are essential to healthy eating, having a high protein content.

The yolk is the most nourishing part of the egg. It contains two proteins, vitellin and livetin, which contain all the essential amino-acids; a high proportion of fat in an emulsified and easily digested form, and lecithin, which is an emulsifier. Also present are Vitamins A, D, B_1 (thiamine), B_2 (riboflavin) and a little nicotinic acid and the minerals iron, calcium and phosphorus. The colour of the yolk depends on the diet of the hen and does not affect the nutritive value.

The white contains less protein (a complex protein called albumin), a little riboflavin, some minerals, which include sulphur, and a high proportion of water.

Eggs contain no Vitamin C and very little carbohydrate, so for a balanced diet they should be served with foods supplying these nutrients.

The energy value of an average egg is 380kJ (90 Kcal).

Composition of an egg	Yolk	White
Protein	16%	13%
Fat	32%	0.25%
Minerals	1%	0.75%
Water	51%	86%

Cholesterol

Eggs are a rich source of cholesterol, which is a 'fat-like' substance produced in the bodies of all animals, including man. Although it is essential to our bodies, we produce sufficient for our own needs, and do not need to eat any more to stay healthy. A high blood cholesterol level is thought to be unhealthy and is one of the conditions often associated with heart disease. In an egg it is the egg yolk which contains the cholesterol and it is advised by experts that those susceptible to heart disease should limit the number of eggs eaten in a week to two, including those used in cooking. It is this high cholesterol content that mars the nutritional magnificence of the egg.

The average cholesterol content of a size 4 egg is 250 mg.

White or brown?

The colour of an egg shell depends entirely on the breed of hen that laid it: whether white or brown, they are equally nutritious.

Free range or factory farmed?

Although many people object to the factory farming of hens, if they have been properly fed their eggs will have the same nutritional value, and with the right diet there will be no difference in flavour.

Quality and grading of eggs

Since 1st February 1973 egg packing in the United Kingdom has been subject to the European Economic Community's agricultural regulations. Three numbers are shown on egg packs, indicating the country of origin, the region of that country and the licence number of the packing station concerned. The number of eggs in the pack, their size and quality classification and the date or week number are also shown.

Quality regulations are subject to the EEC regulations, of which there are three:

Class A eggs: Fresh eggs, naturally clean, intact and internally perfect with a specified size of air cell.

Class B eggs: Second-quality down-graded eggs, including

those with a depth of air cell more than 6mm, but not more than 9mm, preserved and cleaned.

Class C eggs: Eggs not on sale to the public, they are suitable for manufacturing purposes.

A pack of class 'A' eggs with a red band stating the word 'Extra' implies they are 'super-quality', packed in less than seven days with the date of packing clearly stated.

Egg sizes

Size 1	over 70g		
Size 2	65-70g	2¼-2¾oz	Large
Size 3	60-65g		
Size 4	55-60g	1⅔-2¼oz	Standard
Size 5	50-55g		Medium
Size 6	45-50g	1½-1⅔oz	Small
Size 7	under 45g	1½oz	Extra Small

Using eggs in cooking

Most recipes do not specify the size of egg to be used. As a guide, Grades 1, 2 and 3 give similar results and produce a greater volume and are therefore especially useful in cake baking. Grades 4 and 5 are ideal for binding, enriching and glazing but you may have to increase the number of eggs you use in some recipes.

Buying and storing

To ensure freshness, buy your eggs from a shop with a good turnover of produce. Do not buy eggs that have been displayed in the window as light impairs their quality. Ideally, buy in small quantities that will be quickly used. To store, fresh uncracked eggs will keep for several days in a cool place or for up to 3 weeks in a refrigerator at 10°C. Keep them pointed end down so the air space remains uppermost and the yolk is centrally suspended and not in direct contact with the shell, which hastens spoilage.

As the shells are porous eggs readily absorb flavours, so keep them away from strong smelling foods such as cheese, fish or onion.

Freezing eggs

Only shelled raw eggs may be frozen. To freeze whole shelled eggs, place small rigid or waxed paper cases on a baking tray and break an egg into each; cover, freeze, then pack securely in plastic containers.

Egg whites freeze satisfactorily and can even be whisked to stiff peaks after defrosting. Two tablespoons egg white is roughly equivalent to the white of 1 egg.

Egg yolks require the addition of 1 teaspoon sugar or 2 teaspoons salt to every 2 yolks depending on whether they are to be used for savoury or sweet dishes. One tablespoon egg yolk equals 1 egg yolk.

Raw eggs, whole or separated, freeze well for 8 to 10 months.

Thaw eggs in their unopened container at room temperature. Use whole eggs or egg yolks immediately; egg whites will keep up to 2 days if stored in the refrigerator.

Hard-boiled eggs do not freeze successfully, the whites become rubbery.

Coin Purse Eggs, page 65

Storing cracked or separated eggs

To store broken eggs and separated yolks, put into a container with a plastic lid. Add a layer of water to prevent hardening, cover and keep in a cool place. Egg white is best stored in a screw-topped jar. It will keep fresh in the refrigerator for up to 1 week. Broken, separated yolks or cracked eggs should be used within 3 days as the yolk attracts bacteria.

Testing for freshness

There is always a small air space inside an egg and with age this increases. The fresher the egg, therefore, the fuller it is. Use any of the following tests to determine the freshness of eggs.

1. The candling test – hold an egg up to the light. It should be slightly translucent, the air space small and the yolk a pinkish colour with no dark specks showing. If the egg is not fresh the white will appear cloudy, the air space will be larger and the yolk shows as red.

2. Place the eggs in a brine solution. If fresh, it lies flat at the bottom of the glass because it has a small air pocket. If the egg tilts slightly, it is because the air pocket is larger, as the egg has dried out a little. A stale egg rises as it has a large air pocket.

3. On a plate, the yolk of a fresh egg will be domed and surrounded by a thick white layer. A stale egg will be flat (see below).

Should an egg smell bad it should be discarded immediately.

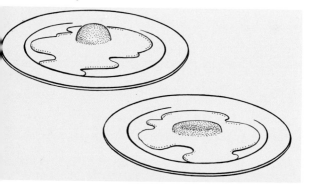

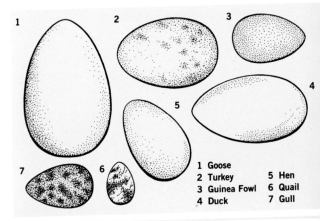

1 Goose
2 Turkey   5 Hen
3 Guinea Fowl 6 Quail
4 Duck   7 Gull

Varieties of eggs

Duck and goose eggs
These are larger than hens' eggs – goose eggs may weigh up to 200 g/7oz – and both can often be purchased from poulterers. They must be thoroughly cooked in order to destroy potentially harmful bacteria. Boil duck eggs for at least 10 minutes and slightly longer for goose eggs. They can be used in cakes and puddings, but not in sponge mixtures or any desserts which cook for only a short time or at a low oven temperature, e.g. meringues.

Quinea fowl eggs
Delicately flavoured small eggs which can be cooked by any method suitable for hens' eggs.

Quail eggs
These are the size of a large cherry and are considered a great delicacy. They are usually hard-boiled and served cold, dressed, on a bed of mustard and cress accompanied by brown bread and butter. It is usual to serve two per portion.

Gull eggs
Available from poulterers; they are unlike most other eggs of sea birds because they do not have a fishy taste. Usually served hard-boiled as an hors d'oeuvre.

Turkey eggs
These are delicately flavoured eggs which are much larger than hens' eggs. Cook and use as for hens' eggs.

Basic Cooking Techniques

Eggs are one of the most versatile ingredients found in the kitchen. They can be prepared as dishes in their own right – scrambled, poached, fried and baked, or blended with other foods to make a wide variety of savoury and sweet dishes.

Often the different properties of an egg are used in a dish, as in flan fillings, the egg whites puff the filling as it cooks and the yolks enrich and thicken the mixture.

Likewise, beaten eggs form a protective coating for fried foods – the albumen quickly hardens on heating and prevents the contents being saturated with fat while the heat penetrates. They also act as binders, the coagulating properties of an egg giving cohesiveness to mixtures containing dry ingredients, for example croquettes, fish cakes, rissoles, etc., and icings. Whisked egg whites incorporate air into mixtures and are used as raising agents for batters and many cakes, while egg yolks have a different effect, both enriching and thickening mixtures, such as sauces and custards. The yolk is also used as an emulsifying agent in mixtures made from oil and butter, for example mayonnaise, Bearnaise and Hollandaise sauce.

Many nourishing and interesting meals can be made from eggs, which are undoubtedly one of the quickest and easiest foods to prepare.

To separate an egg

Sharply knock the middle of the egg once against the side of a bowl – tapping it two or three times is liable to crush the shell and may cause the yolk and white to mix. Use your thumbs to carefully prise the shell in half. Gently pass the yolk back and forth from one half to the other, letting the white drop into the bowl. Use the shell edge to cut off the white and put the yolk into another container.

When separating more than one egg, break each egg over an empty cup before adding to the other yolks and whites in case one of the eggs is bad and spoils the rest. Use the egg shell to scoop out any specks of yolk from the whites.

If you struggle to separate an egg by this method try breaking the egg on to a saucer, hold an egg cup over the yolk and tilt the saucer over a bowl so that the white flows into the bowl and the yolk remains on the saucer.

Whisking egg whites

For best results, egg whites should be at least two to three days old, at room temperature and free from every speck of yolk or grease. Use either a hand-held electric whisk or a balloon whisk for greatest volume, a rotary whisk or electric table-top mixer are fast but the volume will be reduced. Slowly whisk the egg whites until they begin to foam, then increase the speed, and when the egg whites start to stiffen, test the foam. It has reached the 'soft peak stage' when it will hold a drooping peak. To obtain a 'stiff peak' whisk for a few minutes more until the whites will stand up from the whisk in a stiff pyramid. Use the egg whites immediately or they will separate and lose their volume. The egg whites cannot be whisked again.

Folding in egg whites

Use a large metal spoon or spatula and, using a cutting motion, cut down through the whisked egg whites and mixture in which they are to be incorporated and gently roll the egg whites over in a figure-of-eight movement.

If folding whites into a stiff mixture stir in a little of the whisked white before folding in the remainder. This 'softens' the mixture, making it easier to fold in the egg whites without losing too much volume.

Garnishing

Use cold, shelled, hard-boiled eggs. Chop or cut them across into thin slices or lengthways into wedges using a sharp knife or special egg slicer. For a mimosa garnish, sieve the yolks and finely chop the whites and use on vegetable dishes or starters such as egg mayonnaise.

Clarifying consommés and jellies

Lightly beaten egg white and crushed egg shells are used to clarify aspics, consommés and fresh fruit jellies. They are whisked into the hot liquid and form a filter, trapping tiny particles of dirt and grime. This is then removed.

Glazing

Eggs can be used whole or separated as a useful glaze for both sweet and savoury pastry dishes. A pinch of salt helps blend the egg white with the yolk, giving a runnier glaze.

FRIED EGGS

Frying eggs is simplicity itself. Three basic rules apply for cooking fried eggs: use fresh eggs at room temperature so the white of the egg will remain in a firm circle around the yolk, keep the temperature low as eggs scorch easily and fierce heat toughens them (except for deep-fried eggs) and be careful not to overcook them.

To shallow fry eggs

Heat a little butter, bacon fat or oil in a frying pan. Break each egg into a cup and slide it into the pan just before the fat starts to sizzle. The fat should splutter very gently round the eggs: if too hot it will toughen the whites; if not hot enough the whites will not set before the yolks. Spoon the hot fat over the eggs until the whites are set but the yolks are still wobbly, about 3 minutes. Lift out carefully with an egg slice and serve.

Variation

Eggs may be turned over and fried on both sides.

Helpful Hints

Use a good-quality frying pan with a thick base; one with a thin uneven base will cause the eggs to stick and burn. The choice of fat or oil is a personal one, butter gives a good flavour but is expensive, while oil prevents burning. If eggs are to be served with fried bacon, cook this first, then remove the rashers and keep them hot while frying the eggs in the hot bacon fat.

To oven fry eggs

Oven fried eggs or *oeufs sur le plat* are the easiest of all fried eggs to cook. Traditionally, they are cooked and served in shallow, white heatproof dishes with two little handles, but they can be made in any shallow baking dish. The eggs can be cooked on top of the stove if the dishes are flameproof.

Butter individual shallow ovenproof dishes and break 2 eggs into each one then season with salt and pepper. Bake in a preheated moderately hot oven (200°C/400°F, Gas mark 6) for 8 to 10 minutes, or until the whites are just set but the yolks are still runny. Serve immediately.

To deep fry eggs

An exception to the golden rule of frying eggs at low temperatures, deep-fried eggs or *oeuf frit* are a delicious treat of puffy golden fried eggs. Fill a deep-fryer or deep saucepan two-thirds full with oil. Heat the oil to 180°C/350°F. (A cube of bread will brown in about 1 minute at this temperature.)

Break an egg into an oiled ladle and lower into the oil. As soon as the oil bubbles around the egg, remove the ladle quickly or the egg will stick to it. Using a slotted spoon gently roll the egg over once or twice so that the white encloses the yolk. Cook for about 1 minute, until the white is puffed up, crisp and golden. Lift out and drain on crumpled kitchen paper towels. Serve immediately.

Farmhouse Eggs

Metric/Imperial	American
75 g/3 oz butter	¼ cup + 1 tablespoon butter
1 tablespoon oil	1 tablespoon oil
1 kg/2 lb potatoes, peeled and thinly sliced	2 lb potatoes, peeled and thinly sliced
450 g/1 lb onions, peeled and thinly sliced	1 lb onions, peeled and thinly sliced
75 g/3 oz cheese, grated	¾ cup cheese, grated
salt	salt
freshly ground pepper	freshly ground pepper
½ teaspoon dried oregano	½ teaspoon dried oregano
1 teaspoon chopped fresh parsley	1 teaspoon chopped fresh parsley
4 fried eggs	4 fried eggs

Heat 50 g/2 oz (¼ cup) of the butter and the oil in a large frying pan. Add the potatoes and fry gently for 15 to 20 minutes, carefully turning occasionally. Add the onions, cheese, salt and pepper and cook for 10 to 15 minutes, or until cooked, crisp and golden brown. Transfer to a serving dish and keep warm. Beat together the remaining butter, oregano and parsley. Arrange the eggs on the potatoes and top with a dot of herb butter. Serves 4.

POACHED EGGS

A perfect poached egg has the white set neatly around the
yolk and the yolk is soft on the outside and runny inside.

Traditional poached eggs

Poached eggs are one of the most popular breakfast
dishes. With the addition of other ingredients they can also
be transformed into tempting lunch or supper dishes, or an
elegant starter.

Principles

There are two cooking temperatures used when poaching:
a rolling boil when the eggs are added to the water, then
just a simmer to complete cooking. Use only very fresh
eggs (as they are firm and viscous) so the egg white will
hold together in the simmering water. Never add salt to the
poaching water because it breaks down the white, which
will detach itself in strings from the yolk. Instead, add a little
white vinegar, which causes the egg white to seal, because
it decreases the pH, causing coagulation to occur quickly.

To poach eggs

Half-fill a shallow pan with water, add a drop of white
vinegar and bring to the boil. Break each egg into a saucer
and slide it gently into the water. (The water bubbles spin
the egg so that the egg white sets around the yolk.) Reduce
the heat so that the water just simmers and poach the eggs
for 3 to 4 minutes. Lift the eggs out in the order they went
in, using a slotted spoon or slice.

Shaping poached eggs

Eggs can be trimmed to an attractive neat round using a
pastry cutter or by snipping the ragged edges with a pair of
scissors. Poaching rings are also available to help retain
the eggs in a neat round.

Poaching pan

A popular method of poaching eggs is in a metal, cup-
shaped egg poacher. The eggs are not in fact poached as
they are never in contact with the water, but steam-cooked
because the heat is conducted by steam from water in the

metal container through small holes. The pans are heated and buttered before the eggs are put into them and they then take only 3 to 4 minutes to produce lovely buttery eggs, compact in shape.

Helpful Hints

Rinse poached eggs under hot water to remove any vinegary taste.

Eggs can be poached several hours ahead and kept in a bowl of cold water in the refrigerator. To reheat, immerse them in hot water, around 65°C/150°F for 3 to 4 minutes, then drain and pat dry on kitchen paper towels.

Covered poached eggs

The Mediterranean fashion of poaching eggs in flavoured sauces is deliciously different. It is often referred to as 'oven poaching' because the covered dish creates a small oven in which the eggs are cooked by steam generated by other ingredients. The raw eggs are placed on a bed of hot cooked meat or vegetables, covered and cooked on top of the stove or in the oven, until the whites are set and the yolks are soft on the outside and runny inside.

Eggs Florentine and Eggs Benedict, page 16

Eggs Florentine

Metric/Imperial	American
750 g/1½ lb fresh spinach	1½ lb fresh spinach
25 g/1 oz butter	2 tablespoons butter
¼ teaspoon nutmeg	¼ teaspoon nutmeg
salt	salt
freshly ground pepper	freshly ground pepper
4 eggs	4 eggs
Sauce:	*Sauce:*
25 g/1 oz butter	2 tablespoons butter
25 g/1 oz plain flour	¼ cup all-purpose flour
300 ml/½ pt milk	1¼ cups milk
50 g/2 oz cheese, grated	½ cup cheese, grated

Cook the spinach and drain well. Return to the saucepan, add butter, nutmeg, salt and pepper, and keep hot. To make the sauce, melt the butter in a saucepan, add the flour and cook without browning for 2 to 3 minutes. Gradually add the milk, simmer for 2 to 3 minutes, stirring constantly. Stir in half of the cheese, the salt and pepper. Keep hot. Poach the eggs until just set. Put the spinach in an ovenproof dish and arrange the eggs on top. Pour over the sauce, sprinkle with the remaining cheese and brown under a preheated hot grill. Serves 4.

Eggs Benedict

Metric/Imperial	American
25 g/1 oz butter	2 tablespoons butter
8 slices of ham	8 slices of ham
4 muffins	4 muffins
8 poached eggs	8 poached eggs
150 ml/¼ pt Hollandaise Sauce (page 51)	⅔ cup Hollandaise Sauce (page 51)
paprika, to garnish	paprika, to garnish

Melt the butter in a frying pan, add the ham and fry for 2 to 3 minutes. Cut the muffins in half and toast the cut sides only. Put on a serving plate. Top each muffin half with ham and a poached egg. Pour a little warm sauce over each egg and sprinkle with paprika. Serves 4 to 8.

BAKED EGGS

For a quick light lunch or supper or a delicate starter there is nothing more versatile and easy than a baked egg.

All baked egg dishes are cooked until the whites are just set and the yolks still runny. They are best served immediately, as the residual heat from the dish continues to cook the egg after it has been removed from the oven.

There are two main types of baked eggs: *oeufs en cocotte* (eggs in cocotte dishes), baked in small individual dishes with butter and cream; and the more sophisticated *oeufs moulés* (moulded eggs), baked in dariole moulds then turned out on to a circle of fried bread, pastry or a bed of cooked vegetables. These are best served coated with an accompanying sauce. Eggs can be broken into cocotte dishes already containing cooked mixtures to provide additional texture, flavour and interest.

Cocotte Dishes

Traditionally small dishes with curved sides usually large enough to hold one egg are used for baking eggs. Some have one handle, others have small 'ears' at either side. They may be made of porcelain, earthenware or, occasionally, metal. Cocotte dishes are designed to be used as oven to tableware. Ramekin dishes may also be used.

Oeufs en Cocotte

Butter individual cocottes or ramekins. Put 1 tablespoon single cream into each one and drop in 1 or 2 eggs. Season with salt and pepper and put another spoonful of cream or butter on top. Place in a shallow dish of hot water and bake in a preheated moderate oven (180°C/350°F, Gas Mark 4) for 8 to 10 minutes until the whites are just set and the yolks soft. Serve in the dishes.

Variations

For a herby flavour: add 5 ml/1 teaspoon finely chopped fresh tarragon to the cream before pouring it over the egg.

Place 15 ml/1 tablespoon sliced cooked chicken livers, sausages or ham in the base of each dish before adding the egg.

Make a bed of creamed spinach in the base of the cocotte before adding the egg. Serve with a mornay sauce.

Oeufs Moulés

Butter individual dariole moulds. Break an egg into each mould. Place in a shallow dish of hot water and bake in a preheated moderate oven (180°C/350°F, Gas Mark 4) for about 11 minutes until the whites are set and the yolks still runny. To unmould, run a knife carefully between the egg and the edge of mould. Invert the mould, turning the egg on to the chosen base. Serve at once with the sauce.

Helpful Hints

Heat containers before adding the eggs to reduce cooking times. To prevent the egg surface drying out cover with foil or top with breadcrumbs, grated cheese or crushed crisps.

To bake eggs in their shell

It is possible to bake eggs in their shell provided they are at room temperature. Pierce the broad end of the egg with a needle, wrap it in foil and place in a preheated hot oven (220°C/425°F, Gas Mark 7) for 10 minutes (soft yolk) or 20 minutes (hard yolk).

Oeufs en Cocotte Gruyère

Metric/Imperial	American
25 g/1 oz butter	2 tablespoons butter
4 slices Gruyère cheese	4 slices Gruyère cheese
4 eggs	4 eggs
salt	salt
freshly ground pepper	freshly ground pepper
4 tablespoons cream	4 tablespoons cream

Use the butter to grease 4 ramekin dishes and line each with a slice of cheese. Stand the dishes in a baking tin with warm water to come half-way up the dishes. Break an egg into each dish, sprinkle with salt and pepper and spoon over the cream. Cook in a preheated moderate oven (180°C/350°F, Gas Mark 4) for 7 to 10 minutes until the eggs are lightly set. Serves 4 as a starter or supper dish.

Variations

Put one of the following in between the cheese and egg: chopped crispy fried bacon, chopped cooked asparagus tips, or chopped canned artichoke hearts.

Oeufs en Cocotte Gruyère and Country Eggs

Country Eggs

Metric/Imperial
50 g/2 oz butter
3 onions, peeled and sliced
225 g/8 oz skinless
  sausages, cut into
  2.5 cm/1 inch pieces
2 red eating apples, cored
  and sliced
100 g/4 oz streaky bacon,
  rind removed, chopped
salt
freshly ground pepper
4 eggs
chopped fresh parsley, to
  garnish

American
¼ cup butter
3 onions, peeled and sliced
½ lb skinless
  sausages, cut into
  1 inch pieces
2 red eating apples, cored
  and sliced
6 slices streaky bacon, rind
  removed, chopped
salt
freshly ground pepper
4 eggs
chopped fresh parsley, to
  garnish

Melt the butter in a frying pan, add the onions and sausages and cook for about 10 minutes. Add the apples and bacon and fry for a further 5 minutes. Add salt and pepper. Put the mixture into an ovenproof dish, make 4 hollows and break an egg into each. Cook in a preheated moderate oven (180°C/350°F, Gas Mark 4) for 8 to 10 minutes. Sprinkle with parsley before serving with hot crusty bread and butter. Serves 4.

CODDLED EGGS

The term 'coddling' means 'boiling gently', a method that ensures a lightly set egg with a delicate texture. Coddled eggs are ideal for a nourishing breakfast or a simple snack with crusty bread and butter.

Egg Coddlers

Coddlers are heatproof containers usually made of fine porcelain and attractively decorated. They have a lid (usually metal) with a 'lifting ring' attached.

To coddle eggs

Butter the inside of the egg coddler and lid. Break an egg into the coddler and season with salt and pepper. Screw the lid on grasping the whole top firmly (do not use the lifting ring alone). Place the egg coddler up to its neck in a pan of boiling water and simmer for 7 to 8 minutes. Carefully lift from the water, open and serve immediately in the coddler.

Variations

Cheesy eggs Break an egg into the coddler, then sprinkle over 15 g/½ oz (2 tablespoons) soft cheese, cut into 1 cm/½ inch cubes.

Ham Place 1 tablespoon finely chopped ham into the coddler before adding the egg.

Tuna Place 2 tablespoons flaked tuna fish into the coddler before adding the egg.

Mushroom and pâté Place 2 to 3 sliced mushrooms in the bottom of the egg coddler, add salt and pepper. Break in the egg and top with 1 tablespoon pâté.

Helpful Hints

If egg coddlers are not available substitute with a heatproof container and cover tightly with foil.

Always allow the water to simmer gently and never to boil because it will cause the white to coagulate too quickly and become hard.

BOILED EGGS

Probably the simplest method of cooking eggs is boiling – a term that is actually misleading as eggs should only be allowed to simmer and not boil. Perfectly cooked boiled eggs are excellent for breakfast and they form the basis of a multitude of dishes.

Temperature and timing

Boiled eggs should be cooked at simmering point (96°C). At this temperature the white will set firm and the yolk set to a creamy consistency. If the heat is too high, the white will harden before the yolk is set.

Timing is crucial (see chart), as any further cooking after the yolk is set will cause it to become dry and powdery. Overcooking also causes the greenish-black discoloration between the yolk and white of hard-boiled eggs. To prevent this, crack the shell as soon as you remove it from the pan to allow the steam to escape and place immediately under running cold water to cool quickly.

To boil an egg

Traditional method

Place eggs in boiling water to cover. When the water re-boils, turn down to a simmer and count cooking time from then (see chart). Lift the eggs out of the water and tap the shell at one end to prevent further cooking.

Size	Soft	Medium	Hard
45 g/size 6, 7/ small	2 min. 40 sec.	3 min. 20 sec.	7 min.
55 g/size 3, 4, 5/standard	3 min.	3 min. 50 sec.	9 min.
65 g/size 1, 2/ large	3 min. 20 sec.	4 min. 15 sec.	11 min.

There are two other foolproof methods of boiling eggs – so the white sets and is still on the soft side and yet the yolk is slightly runny.

Method 1
Place the eggs in boiling water to cover. When the water reboils, remove the pan from the heat, cover and leave to stand for 9 mins (small eggs), 10 mins (medium eggs) and 11 mins (large eggs). The resulting cooked eggs will have creamy yolks and set whites.

Method 2
Place the eggs in a pan and cover with cold water. Bring the water to the boil gently and remove the eggs from the water as soon as it boils (about 10 to 15 minutes).

Shelling boiled eggs
Gently tap the egg all over to break the shell thoroughly. Carefully peel away a centre band of shell, then slip off the two ends. Rather than pick off any remaining bits of shell, rinse under gently running water.

Helpful Hints
To help prevent cracking, allow the eggs to come to room temperature before plunging into the boiling water. If they are very cold bring them to room temperature in warm water.

Another precaution against cracking is to pierce the broader end of the egg with a pin (or use an egg prick, a little gadget made especially for this purpose). This small hole releases the pressure caused by the sudden increase in temperature as the egg is plunged into the water.

A very fresh egg will take a little longer to boil than one that is a few days old.

If not using immediately plunge cooked eggs into cold water and leave until completely cold. Soft-boiled eggs can be reheated in their shell by immersing them in hot water for 3 to 4 minutes.

Hard-boiled eggs can be kept in the refrigerator (without their shells) for 3 to 4 days; store in a polythene bag.

If an egg cracks during cooking add a little lemon juice or vinegar to the water to help prevent a stream of white escaping into the water.

Use a nylon sieve rather than a metal one when sieving cooked egg yolks otherwise discoloration can occur.

Creole Eggs and Oeufs Chimay, page 24

Creole Eggs

Metric/Imperial	American
6 eggs	6 eggs
25 g/1 oz butter	2 tablespoons butter
4 tablespoons oil	4 tablespoons oil
225 g/8 oz onions sliced	½ lb onions sliced
1 × 400 g/14 oz can tomatoes	1 × 16 oz can tomatoes
salt	salt
freshly ground pepper	freshly ground pepper
2 teaspoons paprika	2 teaspoons paprika
75 g/3 oz cheese, grated	¾ cup cheese, grated

Hard-boil the eggs, shell and slice. Arrange the egg slices in a well greased shallow flameproof dish so they overlap slightly. Heat the oil in a pan, add the onion and fry for 6 to 8 minutes or until soft. Stir in the tomatoes, salt, pepper and paprika. Bring to the boil and simmer for 2 to 3 minutes. Pour over the eggs. Sprinkle over the cheese and put under a preheated grill to heat through and brown the cheese. Serves 4.

Oeufs Chimay

Metric/Imperial	*American*
6 tablespoons oil	6 tablespoons oil
225 g/8 oz onions, peeled and finely chopped	½ lb onions, peeled and finely chopped
100 g/4 oz mushrooms, finely chopped	1 cup mushrooms, finely chopped
salt	salt
freshly ground pepper	freshly ground pepper
½ teaspoon mixed dried herbs	½ teaspoon mixed dried herbs
6 eggs, hard-boiled and shelled	6 eggs, hard-cooked and shelled
Sauce:	*Sauce:*
40 g/1½ oz butter	3 tablespoons butter
25 g/1 oz plain flour	¼ cup all-purpose flour
300 ml/½ pint milk	1¼ cups milk
2 egg yolks	2 egg yolks
50 g/2 oz Cheddar cheese, grated	½ cup Cheddar cheese, grated

Heat the oil in a frying pan, add the onion and fry for 5 to 6 minutes. Add the mushrooms and fry for a further 10 minutes. Add salt, pepper and herbs. Cut the eggs in half lengthways. Remove the yolks and sieve into the onion mixture. Put the mixture into a piping bag with a large star nozzle and pipe a rosette of the mixture into each egg white. Alternatively spoon the mixture into each egg white.

To make the sauce, melt the butter in a saucepan, add the flour and cook for 1 to 2 minutes. Gradually stir in the milk and, stirring constantly, simmer for 2 to 3 minutes. Add salt, pepper and the egg yolks, and simmer for a further 2 to 3 minutes. Do not allow to boil. Arrange the stuffed eggs in a shallow flameproof dish, cover with the sauce and sprinkle over the cheese. Put under a pre-heated grill to heat through and brown. Serve as a supper dish, or as a starter with melba toast. Serves 4.

Variation

Arrange the filled eggs on a bed of cooked brown rice, wholewheat pasta or lightly cooked vegetables before pouring over the sauce.

OMELETTES

An omelette is the exception to the rule that eggs are cooked over a low heat. It is cooked in a few minutes over high heat. There are three types of omelette: the French, the soufflé and the Spanish.

French omelette

This is the most familiar and should be oval-shaped and plump, golden on the outside and creamy inside. The omelette is cooked on one side only, folded and turned out of the pan straight on to the serving dish. Fillings (such as grated cheese or pre-cooked mixtures such as prawns, ham and mushrooms) can be spread across the middle of the omelette before folding it over to serve. French omelettes can also be served cold in brown bread sandwiches or with a salad and they make an impressive dessert, filled with jam or fruit.

Metric/Imperial	*American*
2 eggs	2 eggs
2 teaspoons water	2 teaspoons water
salt	salt
freshly ground pepper	freshly ground pepper
15 g/½ oz butter	1 tablespoon butter

Beat the eggs, water, salt and pepper to taste with a fork. Heat butter in an 18-20 cm/7-8 inch frying pan until it sizzles but do not allow it to brown. Pour in egg mixture, keeping heat high. With a palette knife, draw the mixture from the sides to the middle of the pan and tilt pan so the uncooked egg runs underneath. When the underneath is set but the top still slightly runny, fold the omelette in half (if using 4 eggs, fold the omelette in three). Slide the omelette on to a hot plate. Run a dab of butter on the point of a knife over the top. Garnish and serve at once. Serves 2.

Variations

Cheese Omelette Mix 2 tablespoons grated cheese into the beaten egg mixture.

Omelette Fines Herbes Mix 1 tablespoon chopped mixed fresh herbs into the beaten eggs.

Soufflé Omelette

The most famous variation on the basic French omelette.
The yolks and whites are whisked separately and folded
together just before cooking. The omelette is cooked over
high heat until golden on the underside and then placed
under the grill to finish and the resulting omelette is light
and puffy. They may be sweet or savoury.

Metric/Imperial	*American*
2 eggs, separated	2 eggs, separated
2 teaspoons cold water	2 teaspoons cold water
2 teaspoons caster sugar	2 teaspoons sugar
or salt	or salt
freshly ground pepper	freshly ground pepper
15 g/½ oz butter	1 tablespoon butter

Beat together the egg yolks, water, sugar or salt and
pepper until creamy and light in colour. Whisk the whites
until stiff and fold into the yolk mixture. Melt the butter in an
18-20 cm/7-8 inch omelette pan, pour in the mixture and
cook over a low heat until most of the egg mixture has set
and the underneath is light golden brown. Put the omelette
pan under a preheated hot grill for 1 to 2 minutes to set the
top of the omelette. Fold the omelette in half away from the
pan's handle. Tilt the pan over so that the omelette falls out
on to a serving plate. Serve immediately. Serves 2.
Variations
Jam Spoon warm jam down the centre, fold the omelette
over and dust with caster sugar before serving.
Peppered Prawn Soufflé Omelette Combine 50 g/2 oz
(¼ cup) peeled prawns, 1 teaspoon chilli sauce and 1
tablespoon lemon juice in a small pan and heat through.
Place the warmed filling down the centre of the omelette
and fold in half. Slide on to a heated dish and serve.
Omelette Arnold Bennett Add 3 tablespoons grated
Parmesan cheese and 100 g/4 oz (½ cup) flaked cooked
smoked haddock to the omelette and 4 tablespoons cream
to the egg yolks and add seasoning. Fold in the stiffly
whisked egg white and cook over heat as above. Spoon
over an additional 4 tablespoons cream and brown under a
preheated grill. Serve with a salad.

Spanish Omelette, page 28; and Omelette Arnold Bennett

Omelette pan

One of the keys to success in making the perfect omelette is a good pan. It can be made of aluminium, copper, steel or iron (not enamel as the omelette will stick). The base should be thick to distribute the heat evenly and the sides curved and gently sloping so the omelette can be folded and turned out easily. The size of the pan is important too and needs to be in proportion to the number of eggs used to make the omelette. A 15 cm/6 inch pan is ideal for a 2 or 3 egg omelette and an 18 cm/7 inch pan for 4 or 5 egg omelette.

Omelette pans should be 'proved' before use. To do this, pour in 1 cm/½ inch layer oil and salt. Leave for 12 hours, then heat gently until the oil is very hot and almost smoking. Remove from the heat and leave until cold. Pour off the oil and salt and wipe the pan clean. Ideally the pan should be kept specially for omelettes, which means that you never have to wash it – just wipe the pan with kitchen paper towels dipped in oil and salt.

Spanish Omelette

Far easier to make than the French omelette. It is served flat instead of folded and should be golden brown on both sides and full of mouthwatering extras like bacon and vegetables. The filling is sautéed in a frying pan and the beaten eggs are then poured over and the omelette cooked. Although Spanish omelettes are usually served hot they are also delicious eaten cold as a snack or for a picnic rolled up and placed into hollowed-out loaves.

Metric/Imperial	American
3 tablespoons oil	3 tablespoons oil
100 g/4 oz onions, peeled and thinly sliced	¼ lb onions, peeled and thinly sliced
1 garlic clove, peeled and crushed	1 garlic clove, peeled and crushed
200 g/7 oz cooked potatoes, sliced	½ lb cooked potatoes, sliced
6 eggs	6 eggs
2 tablespoons water	2 tablespoons water
salt	salt
freshly ground pepper	freshly ground pepper

Heat the oil in a large frying pan, add the onion and garlic and cook for 4 to 5 minutes until the onion is soft. Add the potatoes and cook for a further 2 to 3 minutes. Beat together the eggs, water, salt and pepper and pour into the pan. Stir to mix all ingredients together. Leave to cook on a low heat until most of the egg has set, then place the pan under a preheated grill for 2 to 3 minutes. Slide the omelette on to a flat plate for serving. Serves 4.

Variations
Add 1 thinly sliced green pepper to the onion.
Add 2 tomatoes, chopped, with the potatoes.
Sprinkle grated cheese on the omelette before placing it under the grill.

Helpful Hints
Too little heat causes the egg to set unevenly.
Too much stirring after the egg begins to set prevents the base of the omelette from browning.

Luncheon Omelette Cake

Metric/Imperial	*American*
4 tablespoons oil	¼ cup oil
3 courgettes, sliced	3 zucchini, sliced
1 × 325 g/11 oz can broad beans, drained and rinsed	1 × 11 oz can baby lima beans, drained and rinsed
2 ripe medium tomatoes, peeled, seeded and chopped	2 ripe medium tomatoes, peeled, seeded and chopped
1 onion, peeled and thinly sliced	1 onion, peeled and thinly sliced
2 cloves garlic, peeled and crushed	2 cloves garlic, peeled and crushed
2 medium potatoes, cooked, thickly sliced	2 medium potatoes, cooked, thickly sliced
pinch of grated nutmeg	pinch of grated nutmeg
salt	salt
freshly ground pepper	freshly ground pepper
2 tablespoons chopped fresh parsley	2 tablespoons chopped fresh parsley
7 eggs, lightly beaten	7 eggs, lightly beaten

Heat 2 tablespoons oil in a heavy saucepan. Add the vegetables, nutmeg and salt and pepper. Cook gently for 4 to 5 minutes, stirring often, until the onions and courgettes (zucchini) are tender but firm. Stir in the parsley.

Heat the remaining oil in a heavy ovenproof frying pan. Pour the eggs into the pan, add the vegetables, and stir gently. Cook over a medium heat, without stirring, until the bottom of the omelette is set, about 3 to 4 minutes (the top will be still runny).

Put the pan into a preheated hot oven (220°C/425°F, Gas Mark 7) for 6 to 8 minutes, or until the top is brown and puffy. Alternatively, place under a preheated grill to cook and brown the top. Slide the omelette on to a plate and allow to cool. Cut into wedges and serve with a salad. Serves 4 to 6 as hearty main course.

Variations

Add 1 × 200 g/7 oz can salmon or tuna to the eggs cooking in the pan.

SCRAMBLED EGGS

Ideally scrambled eggs should be creamy, smooth-textured and soft enough to almost pour.

There are two basic rules to follow when scrambling eggs: use only fresh eggs at room temperature and keep the cooking temperature low so that the egg thickens gradually and smoothly. Too high a temperature causes some of the egg to set in lumps before the rest of the egg has thickened and the egg mixture will become solid and tough. Do not overcook the eggs — always remove them from the heat before they are fully set as they will continue cooking in their own heat.

Choice of pan

Choose a heavy pan, either a wide saucepan or a deep frying pan preferably non-stick. Whichever you choose, the depth of the liquid egg should be no more than 25 mm/1 inch, so the heat can evenly permeate the egg as it is stirred.

To scramble eggs

Allow 2 eggs per person. Season with salt and freshly ground black pepper and add 1 tablespoon of milk or cream per egg. Beat with a fork until well mixed. Heat a nut of butter in a saucepan, add the eggs and stir with a wooden spoon over a very gentle heat until thick and creamy but a little softer than you would want. Remove from the heat and serve immediately. Serve with mushrooms for a first course or with buttered toast for breakfast.

Variations

Stir about 1 tablespoon of flavouring for every 2 eggs into the uncooked mixture. Try grated cheese, chopped cooked ham or bacon, flaked cooked or smoked fish, crabmeat or prawns.

Pile hot or cold scrambled egg on open sandwiches or in pastry cases and serve as a canapé. For special occasions top with a little caviar.

Scotch Woodcock Pile scrambled egg on to hot buttered toast. Arrange a few anchovy fillets to form a cross on top and put a caper in each quarter.

Eggs with Shrimp Sauce

Metric/Imperial	American
50 g/2 oz butter	¼ cup butter
100 g/4 oz peeled shrimps	½ cup peeled shrimps
2 tablespoons dry white wine	2 tablespoons dry white wine
salt	salt
freshly ground pepper	freshly ground pepper
4 tablespoons double cream	4 tablespoons heavy cream
8 eggs	8 eggs
4 large slices buttered toast	4 large slices buttered toast
chopped fresh parsley, to garnish	chopped fresh parsley, to garnish

Melt half the butter in a small saucepan, add the shrimps, white wine, salt and pepper, and heat gently for 2 to 3 minutes. Stir in the cream and leave on a very low heat. Do not allow the mixture to boil. Beat together the eggs, salt and pepper. Melt the remaining butter in a saucepan, add the eggs, and cook slowly, stirring constantly, until scrambled. Spoon the eggs on to the buttered toast and cover with the shrimp sauce. Sprinkle with parsley and serve as a snack or starter. Serves 4.

SOUFFLES

These delicious egg dishes may be served hot or cold, sweet or savoury. They should always be fluffy and light as air with an open honeycomb texture.

Hot Soufflés

For savoury soufflés the base is usually a béchamel, cream or velouté sauce (panada) combined with a chosen flavouring. Unthickened fish or vegetable purées can also be used on their own. Egg yolks are nearly always added for extra richness. Most sweet soufflés are based on pastry cream (crème pâtissiere) and combined with any one of a variety of flavourings.

This basic mixture should be soft enough to easily fall off a spoon. If it is too thin, the egg whites will be difficult to fold in and if it is too thick the soufflé will be heavy-textured.

The eggs are separated for a soufflé — the yolks are beaten one at a time into the panada so the mixture becomes glossy and elastic. If the panada is too hot when the yolks are added they will coagulate and not expand on heating. If too cool, the yolks will not combine smoothly. The whisked egg whites are added to a soufflé to ensure lightness, and should be at least double the volume of the basic mixture. Make sure the egg whites are at room temperature and free from any trace of yolk. It is best to use a copper bowl with a balloon whisk to incorporate as much air as possible into the mixture.

When making a sweet soufflé whisk the egg whites until stiff then add 1 tablespoon of sugar to every 3 to 4 egg whites and continue whisking for half a minute until glossy, so they become firmer and easier to fold. For a savoury soufflé a pinch of salt or cream of tartar will help the egg whites hold their shape with a soft firmness. Soften the panada mixture by stirring in 1 tablespoon of the stiffly whisked egg white.

Testing the soufflé

If you shake the dish of a cooked soufflé it should tremble slightly, if it quakes all over it is not done. For a firmer texture return the soufflé to the oven until a skewer inserted into the mixture comes out clean.

Folding in egg whites

The stiffly whisked egg whites must be folded into the panada without loss of air from the foam. Combine the two mixtures quickly but lightly, cutting through the mixture with a spatula or large metal spoon, using an over and under motion while rotating the bowl with the other hand. Spoon the mixture into the prepared buttered soufflé dish and level off the top lightly.

A moderately hot oven temperature allows a steady, even rising of the soufflé, so giving maximum volume and stability to the delicate foam. However, if the oven is too hot, the egg will form a skin before it has fully expanded – if too low, rising will be delayed and the soufflé will become close-textured and tough. Set the oven at 190°C/375°F, Gas Mark 5.

When ready, a soufflé should be golden brown and firm on top and should have increased in size by half or two-thirds its volume and risen above the rim of the dish. Once cooked it must be served immediately otherwise it will collapse as steam escapes. It is served with two spoons breaking the crust and spooning into the centre so each person has some of the outside crust and some of the creamy centre.

Soufflé dish

Originally, soufflés were cooked in pastry cases that were similar to straight-sided dishes. The classic soufflé dish is made of white ovenproof porcelain with straight sides, but earthenware, ovenproof glass and metal can also be used. Dishes vary in size from 150 ml/¼ pint (⅔ cup) for an individual serving to about 2 litres/3½ pint (9 cups) for 8 people.

If a soufflé dish is unavailable use a charlotte mould or any deep, heatproof dish.

Cheese Soufflé

Metric/Imperial	*American*
40 g/1½ oz butter	3 tablespoons butter
3 tablespoons flour	3 tablespoons flour
250 ml/8 fl oz warm milk	1 cup warm milk
40 g/1½ oz Parmesan cheese, freshly grated	⅓ cup freshly grated Parmesan cheese
salt	salt
freshly ground pepper	freshly ground pepper
pinch of cayenne pepper	pinch of cayenne pepper
pinch of grated nutmeg	pinch of grated nutmeg
4 egg yolks	4 egg yolks
5 egg whites	5 egg whites
½ teaspoon cream of tartar	½ teaspoon cream of tartar

Butter an 18 cm/7 inch soufflé dish. Put the dish on a baking sheet. Melt the butter in a saucepan, add the flour and cook over a low heat for 1 minute. Remove from the heat, cool a little, then blend in the milk, stirring until smooth. Return to the heat and stir until boiling, then take from the heat and stir in the cheese and seasonings. Beat in the egg yolks, one at a time. Whisk the whites with cream of tartar until firm but not brittle and fold into the cheese mixture.

Pour the mixture into the prepared dish, tap the bottom of the dish lightly on the work surface to expel any large air pockets, and smooth the top of the soufflé. Quickly run a knife around the top of the mixture about 2.5 cm/1 inch from the edge to make the soufflé rise evenly in a crown. Immediately place the dish in a preheated moderately hot oven (190°C/375°F, Gas Mark 5) for about 24 minutes, until puffed up, golden brown on top and just firm. Serve at once as a first course or light luncheon dish. Serves 4.

Variations

Blue Cheese Use Stilton instead of Parmesan cheese.

Fish soufflé Add 50-75 g/2-3 oz cooked flaked haddock, crab or salmon in place of the cheese.

Ham soufflé Add 50 g/2 oz (¼ cup) chopped cooked ham with the cheese.

Mushroom soufflé Add 75-100 g/3-4 oz (1 cup) sliced mushrooms, sautéed in a little butter with the cheese.

Hot Sweet Soufflé

Hot Sweet Soufflé

Metric/Imperial	*American*
90 g/3½ oz butter	7 tablespoons butter
50 g/2 oz plain flour	½ cup all-purpose flour
300 ml/½ pint milk	1¼ cups milk
50 g/2 oz caster sugar	¼ cup sugar
1 teaspoon vanilla essence	1 teaspoon vanilla
4 eggs, separated	4 eggs, separated
2 teaspoons icing sugar	2 teaspoons confectioners' sugar

Use the 15 g/½ oz (1 tablespoon) butter to grease a 1 litre/2 pint (1 quart) soufflé dish. Put the dish on a baking sheet. Melt the butter in a saucepan, add the flour and cook for 2 to 3 minutes. Gradually stir in the milk and, stirring constantly, simmer for 2 to 3 minutes. Stir in the sugar and vanilla essence. Allow to cool slightly and add the egg yolks, one at a time, beating well after each addition. Whisk the egg whites until stiff and fold into the mixture. Pour into the prepared dish and cook in a preheated moderately hot

oven (190°C/375°F, Gas Mark 5) for 35 to 40 minutes.
Sprinkle with icing sugar and serve. Serves 4.
Variations
Lemon soufflé Add the finely grated rind of 2 lemons and
the juice of 1 lemon after the sauce has come to the boil.
Orange soufflé Add the finely grated rind and juice of 1
orange after the sauce has come to the boil. Serve the
cooked soufflé with a vanilla sauce.
Chocolate soufflé Dissolve 50-75g/2-3oz (½ cup) plain
chocolate in the milk and omit the vanilla essence.
Coffee soufflé Add 2 teaspoons coffee essence to the milk.
Serve the soufflé with brandy flavoured whipped cream.
Liqueur soufflé Add 3 tablespoons of any liqueur after the
egg yolks have been added to the sauce.
Almond soufflé Simmer 75g/3oz (¾ cup) flaked almonds,
150ml/¼ pint (⅔ cup) milk and 2 teaspoons caster sugar for
40 minutes. Blend until smooth then add 100ml/3floz
Amaretto di Saronno. Fold into the mixture with the egg
yolks.
Individual soufflés Use individual serving dishes and bake
for only 18 minutes.

Cold Soufflés
Cold soufflés should not be confused with the hot version,
as they are really mousses which are set with gelatine in a
soufflé dish lined with a paper collar. This is then removed
and the 'puffed-up' mixture resembles a true soufflé. Cold
sweet soufflés have a custard base into which whipped
cream and whisked egg whites are folded.

To prepare a soufflé dish
Cut a band of double
greaseproof paper long
enough to overlap by
5cm/2 inches round the
dish and wide enough to
stand 8cm/3 inches above
it. Grease the inside of the
dish and the top half of the
paper band. Wrap it round
the outside of the dish with
the fold at the base and
secure with string.

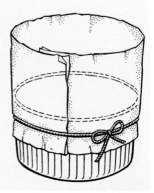

Fresh Orange and Lemon Soufflé

Metric/Imperial	American
3 eggs, separated	3 eggs, separated
175 g/6 oz caster sugar	2/3 cup + 2 tablespoons sugar
100 ml/4 fl oz orange juice	1/2 cup orange juice
50 ml/2 fl oz lemon juice	1/4 cup lemon juice
12 g/1/2 oz powdered gelatine	2 envelopes unflavored gelatin
300 ml/1/2 pint whipping cream	1 1/4 cups whipping cream
2 tablespoons Orange Curaçao, Cointreau or Grand Marnier (optional)	2 tablespoons Orange Curaçao, Cointreau or Grand Marnier (optional)
To decorate:	To decorate:
crystallized orange and lemon slices	crystallized orange and lemon slices
pistachio nuts or angelica	pistachio nuts or angelica
double cream (optional)	heavy cream (optional)

Prepare a 15 cm/6 inch soufflé dish. Whisk the egg yolks, sugar and fruit juice in a large bowl over a saucepan of boiling water (take care the water does not touch the bowl), until the mixture is thick and foamy and falls from the whisk in ribbons on to the mixture. Remove from the heat.

Dissolve the gelatine in a cup with 3-4 tablespoons boiling water. When thoroughly dissolved, whisk into the fruit mixture. Set aside to chill and thicken. Whisk the egg whites until thick but not brittle. Whip the cream to a soft peak. When the fruit mixture has thickened and is beginning to set, fold in the cream and then the egg whites, then fold in the liqueur. Turn the mixture into the soufflé dish, smooth the top and refrigerate until set. Peel off the paper collar with the help of a knife dipped in hot water. Cut the orange and lemon slices into small wedges, halve or chop the pistachio nuts or angelica and decorate to taste, using whipped cream if liked.

Variation

Fresh Grapefruit Soufflé Use 100 ml/4 fl oz (1/2 cup) grapefruit juice and 50 ml/2 fl oz (1/4 cup) orange juice instead of lemon.

BATTERS

Batters provide the basis for a wide number of dishes from simple toad-in-the-hole to Russian blini, French crêpes and Chinese rolled pancakes.

A batter is a mixture of flour, salt, egg, milk or other liquid. The proportions vary, depending on the consistency required: pancakes should have a thin, cream-like consistency, while fritters need a thick coating batter.

Pancakes (crêpes)

Eggs give richness and flavour to pancakes as well as binding the mixture together in the pan. Usually white flour is used, though buckwheat or wholemeal flour are just as suitable. Sometimes the milk is replaced with Cognac, wine or beer (which lightens the mixture). Salt seasons the batter, but for a sweet pancake sugar can be added.

The batter must not be overbeaten as the resulting pancakes will be tough. Aim for the consistency of thin cream as the lighter and thinner the batter the more delicate the pancake will be. A good pancake is easily recognized as it is paper thin with a marbled surface where it has browned in the pan.

The pancake (crêpe) pan

If possible keep a separate pan for pancakes. Like omelette pans, crêpe pans should never be washed. Simply wipe them thoroughly with a cloth or kitchen paper towels after use while still hot. Choose a pan with a diameter of 15 cm/6 inches, which is heavy enough to distribute the heat evenly yet light enough to handle easily. Rounded sides are an advantage.

Greasing the pan is most important. The pan must be made very hot first, then wipe the bottom with oil or clarified butter, swirling it around the bottom and sides to coat evenly. Repeat after every pancake.

Stacking pancakes

To keep pancakes warm, either stack them in a low oven, which makes them slightly crisp, or on an upturned plate over a pan of hot water, covering them with a clean, folded towel to keep them tender.

Basic Pancake Batter

Metric/Imperial	*American*
125 g/4 oz plain flour	1 cup all-purpose flour
½ teaspoon salt	½ teaspoon salt
1 egg	1 egg
350 ml/12 fl oz milk	1½ cups milk
15 g/½ oz butter, melted	1 tablespoon butter, melted

Sift the flour and salt into a mixing bowl. Make a well in the centre and add the egg, milk and butter. Gradually mix in the flour. Beat well, cover and leave to stand for 1 hour. Heat a little butter in a pan. Use a small jug to pour in enough batter to coat the surface of the pan (or use about 2 tablespoons batter for a 15 cm/6 inch pan). Tilt the pan to run the batter smoothly and evenly over the surface. Cook until small bubbles appear, about 1 minute, then turn the pancake over with a spatula. Cook for 1 minute on the other side, or until set and golden brown. Lift out of the pan and stack. Repeat the process for each pancake. Makes about 14 pancakes.

Prawn and Cheese Pancakes, page 40

Fillings for Rolled Pancakes (Crêpes)

Quantities given here are enough to fill 8 pancakes (crêpes) 15 cm/6 inches in diameter.

Prawn and Cheese Fold 250 g/8 oz (1 cup) cooked and drained prawns with 50 g/2 oz (½ cup) soured cream, 2 tablespoons chopped parsley and 25 g/1 oz (¼ cup) grated Cheddar cheese. Season with pepper and grated nutmeg. Fill the pancakes and arrange in an ovenproof serving dish. Pour hot cheese sauce over, sprinkle with 1 teaspoon sesame seeds and bake in a preheated hot oven (200°C/400°F, Gas Mark 6) for 20 minutes.

Crab or Chicken Bengal Sauté 2 finely chopped spring onions in 25 g/1 oz (2 tablespoons) butter. Stir in 2 teaspoons curry powder, fry for 1 minute, then add ½ teaspoon Worcestershire sauce, a dash of Tabasco, 4 tablespoons each soured cream and plain yogurt and salt to taste. Fold in 250 g/8 oz (1 cup) crabmeat or chopped, cooked chicken and heat gently. Fill the pancakes with the hot mixture and arrange in a flameproof serving dish. Spread with a little cream and place under a hot grill to glaze.

Cherry Sprinkle 1 tablespoon Kirsch over 75 g/3 oz canned or stewed black cherries. Mix with 25 g/1 oz (¼ cup) slivered almonds and fill the pancakes (crêpes) as usual. Arrange in an ovenproof serving dish, sprinkle well with caster sugar and place in a preheated moderately hot oven (200°C/400°F, Gas Mark 6) for 3 to 4 minutes until the sugar forms a glaze. Serve with chilled whipped cream.

To store pancakes

If you want to cook pancakes in advance, cool them on a wire rack and when cold, stack, separated by rounds of greaseproof paper or cling film. Pack closely in manageable quantities of 8 to 12 in a polythene bag. Refrigerate for up to five days or freeze for up to four months.

To re-heat pancakes

Thaw frozen pancakes, unwrapped, at room temperature for 2 hours or overnight in a refrigerator. Alternatively place the stacked pancakes on an upturned plate and place over a pan of hot water and cover with a bowl. Stuff pancakes and reheat in the oven until the filling is hot.

Basic batter

Follow the method given for basic pancake batter and use to make crisp, golden Yorkshire puddings or humble toad-in-the-hole.

Metric/Imperial
125 g/4 oz plain flour
pinch of salt
1 egg
300 ml/½ pint milk

American
1 cup all-purpose flour
pinch of salt
1 egg
1¼ cups milk

Yorkshire pudding

Brush Yorkshire pudding (muffin) tins generously with melted butter or dripping and place them in a preheated hot oven (220°C/425°F, Gas Mark 7) for a few minutes until the fat begins to smoke. Remove from the oven, stir the batter and pour in quickly to fill each tin two-thirds full. Bake in the oven for 15 to 20 minutes or until well risen, crisp and golden brown. Serve immediately as an accompaniment to roast beef. Makes 12.

Variation

Make one large pudding and cut into squares. In this case, heat 2 or 3 tablespoons of dripping in a 25×23×5 cm/10×9×2 inch baking tray and bake as above.

Toad-in-the-Hole

Make basic batter. Put 8 large sausages into a small roasting tin or baking dish about 25×23×5 cm/10×9×2 inches and bake in a preheated hot oven (220°C/425°F, Gas Mark 7) for 7 to 8 minutes, turning two or three times until browned all over. Arrange the sausages evenly spaced in the dish, stir the batter and pour it over. Bake in the oven for 20 to 30 minutes or until well risen, crisp and golden brown. Serve immediately. Serves 4.

Fritters

There are endless variations to the fritter, but they should all puff up to a light, golden crispness while the enclosed food stays soft and succulent. The fritter batter must be thick in order to coat the food without running off – dipping the food in flour first helps the batter to stick.

Basic fritter batter

Metric/Imperial	*American*
125 g/4 oz plain flour	1 cup all-purpose flour
pinch of salt	pinch of salt
150 ml/¼ pint milk	⅔ cup milk
1 egg yolk	1 egg yolk
25 g/1 oz butter, melted	2 tablespoons butter, melted
2 egg whites, stiffly beaten	2 egg whites, stiffly beaten

Sift the flour and salt into a mixing bowl and make a well in the centre. Add half the milk and the egg yolk and gradually mix in the flour with a wooden spoon. When the mixture becomes very stiff, gradually add the remaining milk, beating well between each addition, to make a very thick batter. Stir in the melted butter and fold in the stiffly beaten egg whites. Makes about 300 ml/½ pint (1¼ cups) fritter batter.

Use to coat onion rings, potato matchsticks, cauliflower sprigs, slices of pepper, chopped cooked chicken and deep-fry until puffed up golden brown and crisp.

Buckwheat Blini

Crisp, light, yeast-raised blini are the Russian version of pancakes, traditionally served as an hors d'oeuvre with caviar, soured cream, pickled herring and smoked salmon; they make an unusual dish for a buffet or a cocktail party.

Metric/Imperial	*American*
300 ml/½ pint milk	1¼ cups milk
10 g/¼ oz fresh yeast	¼ oz compressed yeast
50 g/2 oz plain flour	½ cup all-purpose flour
½ tablespoon sugar	½ tablespoon sugar
65 g/2½ oz butter	½ cup + 1 tablespoon butter
1 egg, separated	1 egg, separated
¼ teaspoon salt	¼ teaspoon salt
175 g/6 oz buckwheat flour	1½ cups buckwheat flour
melted butter	melted butter

Buckwheat Blini

Warm half of the milk and blend with the yeast. Sift the flour into a large bowl and stir in the sugar. Gradually beat in the yeast mixture. Cover with a cloth and leave in a warm place to rise for about 1 to 1½ hours, until double in size. Melt 15g/½oz (1 tablespoon) butter, and beat into the risen mixture with the egg yolk and salt. Stir in the buckwheat flour. Warm the remaining milk and gradually beat into the mixture. Cover with a cloth and leave to rise again in a warm place for about 1 hour, or until double in size. Whisk the egg white until stiff and fold into the mixture.

Melt 15g/½oz (1 tablespoon) of the remaining butter in a frying pan and add tablespoons of the mixture to make small pancakes. Cook for 2 to 3 minutes until set, then turn over and cook a further 2 to 3 minutes until cooked and golden brown.

Remove the pancakes from the pan, drain on kitchen paper towels and keep warm between 2 plates over a pan of hot water. Continue heating a little butter and making batches of pancakes until all the mixture has been used. Place the pancakes on a serving plate and pour on some melted butter. Serve with separate dishes of caviar, smoked salmon, pickled herring and soured cream. Makes about 24 pancakes.

MERINGUES

Meringue is easy to make provided a few points are observed – the bowl and whisk must be clean and dry. Any grease or egg yolk present will prevent the egg whites from whisking to their full volume. Use eggs at room temperature.

The shape of the whisk and bowl also influence a good meringue; a wire balloon whisk or spiral whisk gives the greatest volume, but takes longer than a rotary whisk. An electric mixer is the quickest, but gives the least volume. Choose a wide bowl when using a balloon whisk and a narrow, deep bowl for a rotary hand whisk.

Meringues are best cooked on non-stick (parchment) paper or rice paper, but a thoroughly greased and floured baking tray can be used.

Use fine sugar for meringues; caster sugar is generally used, but equal quantities of caster and icing sugar can be used. Do not use granulated sugar, the sugar crystals reduce the volume.

There are three types of meringue: Meringue Suisse, Meringue Italienne and cooked meringue, or Meringue Cuite. They are all usually shaped then cooked in a very cool oven until dry (see below).

Meringue Suisse

Simplest of all meringues to make, it must be baked immediately it is made.

Metric/Imperial	American
4 egg whites	4 egg whites
250 g/8 oz caster sugar	1 cup sugar

Whisk the egg whites in a large bowl until very stiff and dry, then add the sugar 1 tablespoon at a time, whisking thoroughly between each addition. The meringue should be glossy and form soft peaks. For a more open-textured meringue, whisk in half the sugar and fold in the remainder with a wire whisk or metal spoon. Use immediately to shape shells, rounds or baskets and bake in a preheated very cool oven (120°C/250°F, Gas Mark ½) until dry. Or use to top puddings and bake in a moderate oven (180°C/350°F, Gas Mark 3) for 15 to 20 minutes.

Meringue Italienne

Metric/Imperial
3 tablespoons water
250 g/8 oz caster sugar
3 egg whites, stiffly whisked
½ teaspoon vanilla
  essence

American
3 tablespoons water
1 cup sugar
3 egg whites, stiffly whisked
½ teaspoon vanilla

Place the water and sugar in a heavy-based pan over a low heat until the sugar has dissolved and the liquid is clear. Increase the heat and boil rapidly until 150°C/300°F shows on a sugar thermometer, or until a small amount dropped into cold water can be rolled into a hard ball. Pour the syrup into the whisked egg whites in a slow thin stream, whisking continuously to form a thick glossy meringue. Whisk in the vanilla essence. Pipe into small meringues the size of a walnut and bake in a very cool oven (120°C/250°F, Gas Mark ½) until dry. Or use as a cake filling and topping.

Meringue Cuite

Metric/Imperial
4 egg whites
250 g/8 oz icing sugar,
  sifted
½ teaspoon vanilla
  essence

American
4 egg whites
1¾ cups sifted
  confectioners' sugar
½ teaspoon vanilla

Place all the ingredients in a large mixing bowl over a pan of simmering water. Whisk with rotary or wire whisk for about 10 minutes, until the mixture is very thick and glossy and forms soft but well-shaped peaks. Remove the bowl from the heat and continue whisking until the bowl is cool enough to touch. Use and bake as for Meringue Suisse.

Helpful Hints
Uncooked Meringue Italian can be kept for up to a week in a covered container in the refrigerator.

All baked meringues keep well for several weeks in an airtight container. They can be frozen for up to 3 months. Dry out soft meringues in a very low oven.

Peach Meringue Pie

Meringues Chantilly

Metric/Imperial	*American*
2 large egg whites	2 large egg whites
50 g/2 oz caster sugar	¼ cup sugar
Filling:	*Filling:*
120 ml/4 fl oz double cream	½ cup heavy cream
1 teaspoon caster sugar	1 teaspoon sugar
few drops vanilla essence	few drops of vanilla

Line a baking sheet with non-stick (parchment) paper. Make the meringue as described in Meringue Suisse using the egg whites and sugar. Shape the meringues by taking 2 soup or serving spoons and, with one, scoop up a heaped spoonful of the mixture. With the other spoon, scoop the meringue out on to the baking tray to form a half-egg shape. Neaten with a knife dipped in cold water. Alternatively, pipe the meringue using a large plain or rose nozzle. Dredge with sugar and bake in a preheated very cool oven (120°C/250°F, Gas Mark ½) for about 1 hour until a delicate beige colour. Peel the paper off the meringues. Gently press the base of each meringue, while still warm, to make a hollow. Replace upside down on the sheet and return to the oven for a further 30 minutes to complete cooking. Cool on a wire rack. An hour or two before required, whip the cream with the sugar and vanilla until stiff, and sandwich pairs of meringues together.

Peach Meringue Pie

Metric/Imperial	American
4 egg whites	4 egg whites
250 g/8 oz caster sugar	1 cup sugar
120 ml/4 fl oz double cream	½ cup heavy cream
about 250 g/8 oz fresh or canned peaches, sliced	1 cup sliced fresh or canned peaches
chopped pistachio nuts, to decorate	chopped pistachio nuts, to decorate

Line a baking sheet with non-stick (parchment) or grease-proof paper. Draw on it in pencil two circles 18 cm/7 inches in diameter. Lightly grease with melted lard or oil. Make meringue as for Meringue Suisse.

Fit a large plain or rose nozzle into a forcing bag and fill it with meringue. Pipe a ring of meringue round one circle just inside the pencilled line. Pipe on to the paper 8 to 12 baby rosettes with bases the same width as the meringue ring. Pipe the remaining mixture into the other circle and spread it evenly into a flat disc. Bake the meringue in a preheated cool oven (140°C/275°F, Gas Mark 1) for 1 hour or until crisp when tapped. Remove from the oven, lift off the rosettes with a thin knife and place on a rack. Turn the paper upside down and carefully peel off the meringue ring and disc. Carefully place on to a rack to cool.

Shortly before serving, whip the cream until stiff and spoon into a forcing bag fitted with a 1 cm/½ inch rose nozzle. Place the meringue disc on the serving plate and pipe a ring of cream round the edge. Set the meringue ring on top and press down gently. Arrange the peach slices inside the ring in concentric circles. Pipe a little cream on the base of each rosette and arrange on the ring, pressing each down gently to secure. Pipe the remaining cream in rosettes round the ring to decorate, and top with chopped pistachio nuts. Chill until serving time (up to 2 hours).

Variations

Instead of peaches use fresh raspberries, strawberries or other fresh or canned and well drained fruit such as plums or apricots.

Use toasted flaked almonds, chopped walnuts, or hazelnuts instead of pistachio nuts.

EGG CUSTARDS

There are two types of egg-based custard: baked or
steamed, and the smooth pouring custard which is used as
a sauce.

Custards can be thickened either exclusively with eggs
or with the addition of a starch like flour, cornflour, potato
flour or arrowroot. A custard thickened solely by eggs is
much more delicate – too much heat or rapid change in
temperature causes the eggs to curdle. The custard therefore must be protected from the direct heat so that its
temperature rises gradually. An egg custard cooked on top
of the stove should be made in a double saucepan (if this is
not available use an ordinary saucepan over very gentle
heat). Baked custards should be placed in a bain-marie:
place the dish containing the custard in a fairly deep cake
tin or roasting pan and pour in sufficient hot water to come
half-way up the sides of the dish.

Custard Sauce

Metric/Imperial	American
600 ml/1 pint milk	2½ cups milk
½ vanilla pod	½ vanilla bean
2 tablespoons caster sugar	2 tablespoons sugar
4 egg yolks	4 egg yolks

Put the milk and vanilla pod (vanilla bean) into a saucepan
and heat gently to scalding point. Remove the pan from the
heat, cover and leave to infuse for 10 minutes. Remove the
vanilla pod (vanilla bean) and stir in the sugar. Whisk the
egg yolks in a bowl and gradually blend in the milk. Strain
the custard back into the saucepan or into a double saucepan with hot, but not boiling water in the base. Stir the
custard until the sauce coats the back of a wooden spoon.
Serve hot or cold. Makes 600 ml/1 pint (2½ cups) custard.
Serving the custard
To serve hot, strain through a fine sieve into a bowl or jug
and serve immediately. To serve cold, strain into a jug or
bowl and leave to cool, stirring once or twice to prevent a
skin forming. Cover the surface of the cooled custard with a
piece of lightly buttered greaseproof paper, then chill in the

refrigerator. Alternatively, sprinkle the custard with sugar to stop a skin forming and stir just before serving.

To rescue a curdled custard

Custard has curdled when you see a faint watery texture and soft lumps forming around the edge. Turn the custard into a cold bowl and whisk hard.

Note

To eliminate the danger of curdling, blend 1 teaspoon cornflour with the egg yolks.

Baked Egg Custard

Metric/Imperial	*American*
15-25 g/½-1 oz butter	1-2 tablespoons butter
600 ml/1 pint milk	2½ cups milk
strip of lemon or orange rind	strip of lemon or orange rind
2 whole eggs	2 whole eggs
2 egg yolks	2 egg yolks
1½ tablespoons caster sugar	1½ tablespoons sugar
grated nutmeg	grated nutmeg

Butter the inside of a 900 ml/1½ pint (5 to 6 cup) soufflé dish. Put the milk and lemon or orange rind into a saucepan and bring to just below boiling point, remove from the heat. In a basin beat together the eggs, egg yolks and sugar. Pour the milk over the egg mixture, stir, then strain the mixture into the soufflé dish. Sprinkle over the nutmeg and stand the dish in a baking tin with warm water to come half-way up the dish. Cook in a preheated moderate oven (180°C/350°F, Gas Mark 4) for about 35 minutes or until the custard is set and the top golden brown. Serve warm or cold. Serves 4.

To test a baked egg custard
Insert the point of a sharp knife into the centre of the custard. If it is ready a visible mark will be left, if it flows together, cook for a little longer.

EGG SAUCES

Egg sauces are made from egg yolks and a high proportion of butter or oil; whisked together, they emulsify to form a thick and creamy consistency.

Mayonnaise, page 53; Hollandaise and Béarnaise Sauce

Béarnaise Sauce

Metric/Imperial	*American*
25 g/1 oz chopped shallot	¼ cup chopped challot
6 peppercorns	6 peppercorns
1 tablespoon tarragon vinegar	1 tablespoon tarragon vinegar
2 egg yolks	2 egg yolks
25 g/1 oz softened butter	2 tablespoons softened butter
salt	salt
freshly ground pepper	freshly ground pepper
juice of ½ lemon	juice of ½ lemon
2 teaspoons chopped fresh tarragon	2 teaspoons chopped fresh tarragon
1 teaspoon chopped fresh chervil	1 teaspoon chopped fresh chervil

Put the shallots, peppercorns and vinegar into a saucepan, boil to reduce to half quantity, strain into a heatproof basin and allow to cool. Add the egg yolks and whisk over a saucepan of hot water over a low heat, until pale in colour and thick enough to coat the back of a wooden spoon. Gradually whisk in the butter then remove the basin from the heat. Stir in the salt, lemon juice, tarragon and chervil. Serve with steaks and grilled meat. Makes about 150 ml/¼ pint (⅔ cup).

Hollandaise Sauce

Metric/Imperial	American
2 tablespoons wine vinegar	2 tablespoons wine vinegar
2 tablespoons water	2 tablespoons water
3 egg yolks	3 egg yolks
125 g/4 oz softened butter, cut into pieces	½ cup softened butter, cut into pieces
2 tablespoons lemon juice	2 tablespoons lemon juice
salt	salt
freshly ground pepper	freshly ground pepper

Boil the vinegar in a saucepan until reduced by half. Add the water and pour into a heatproof basin. Add the egg yolks, put the basin over a saucepan of hot water on a low heat, and whisk continuously until thick enough to coat the back of a wooden spoon. Gradually whisk in the butter, then the lemon juice, salt and pepper to taste. Serve the sauce warm with fish, chicken, asparagus or broccoli. Makes about 175 ml/6 fl oz (¾ cup).

Variations

Mousseline Sauce Whip 3 to 4 tablespoons double cream until stiff. Fold into the Hollandaise Sauce and season with salt to taste. Serve immediately with asparagus, poached or grilled fish and chicken.

Blender or Food Processor Hollandaise Place 3 egg yolks, 1 teaspoon lemon juice and 1 tablespoon water into the container and blend briefly. Heat 125 g/4 oz (½ cup) butter until just melted, but not separated. With the motor at high speed, pour the butter very slowly into the container. Season with more lemon juice and salt and pepper to taste.

Helpful Hints

If the sauce separates it is usually because it is too hot. To rescue a curdled sauce, remove at once from the heat and whisk in an ice cube. If this is not successful, rinse another bowl with hot water, dry it and put in a teaspoon of lemon juice, an egg yolk and a tablespoon of sauce. Whisk together with a fork or wire whisk until they thicken, then gradually whisk in the remaining sauce initially only adding a drop at a time.

Occasionally a sauce can curdle because it is too cool and has not been sufficiently cooked. Bring a tablespoon of water to the boil, then whisk in the separated sauce drop by drop over a low heat.

Hot egg sauces can be kept warm by placing the bowl over a saucepan of hot water, or by standing the saucepan in a pan of hot water. Do not use any heat.

Cook hot egg sauces slowly and gently, sudden heat causes them to curdle.

Sabayon Sauce

Sabayon Sauce is a sweet emulsified sauce which is made rather like Hollandaise by whisking egg yolks with a liquid (usually white wine) and sugar to a light fluffy mousse that is thin enough to pour.

Metric/Imperial	American
4 egg yolks	4 egg yolks
50 g/2 oz caster sugar	¼ cup sugar
150 ml/¼ pint dry white wine	⅔ cup dry white wine
grated rind of 1 orange or 1 lemon (optional)	grated rind of 1 orange or 1 lemon (optional)

Put the egg yolks, sugar and wine into a heatproof basin and whisk over a saucepan of hot water over a low heat, until the sauce is frothy and almost thick enough to leave a trail. Add the grated orange or lemon rind if using. If serving the sauce warm, serve immediately. If serving the sauce cold, continue whisking until cold, then set over a bowl of iced water. Do not leave for more than 1 hour. Serve with poached fruits. Also excellent with Christmas pudding. Makes about 8 fl oz/250 ml (1 cup)

Mayonnaise

Metric/Imperial	American
2 egg yolks	2 egg yolks
½ teaspoon salt	½ teaspoon salt
pinch of white pepper	pinch of white pepper
½ teaspoon dry mustard	½ teaspoon dry mustard
2 teaspoons wine or cider vinegar, or lemon juice	2 teaspoons wine or cider vinegar, or lemon juice
250 ml/8 fl oz olive or other vegetable oil	1 cup olive or other vegetable oil

Rinse a small bowl in hot water, dry it and wrap the base in a damp cloth to keep it steady. Add the egg yolks, seasonings and 1 teaspoon vinegar or lemon juice. Beat together, then add the oil, drop by drop, from a teaspoon at first, then trickle in from a jug. Stir vigorously and constantly in one direction. Incorporate each addition thoroughly before adding the next. If the mixture shows signs of separating, beat in a teaspoon of boiling water before adding more oil. When all the oil is incorporated, beat in the remaining vinegar or lemon juice. Adjust the seasoning. Makes about 250 ml/8 fl oz (1 cup).

Variations

Blender or Food Processor Mayonnaise Place the egg yolks, seasonings, and 1 teaspoon vinegar or lemon juice in the container and process for a few seconds. With the motor running, pour the oil in little by little, checking that each addition is absorbed before adding the next; then add the remaining vinegar or lemon juice.

Aioli Crush 3 cloves garlic and add to the egg yolks with seasoning.

Curry Mayonnaise Add 1 teaspoon curry powder to the egg yolks before adding the oil.

Herb Mayonnaise Add 2 tablespoons chopped fresh chives and 1 tablespoon chopped fresh parsley.

To rescue curdled mayonnaise

In a warm bowl, whisk the curdled mayonnaise drop by drop into any of the following: a few drops of warm water, a few drops of vinegar, a little mustard or another egg yolk (if using another egg yolk you may need to add extra oil).

Oeufs Provençal and Hidden Eggs

Oeufs Provençal

Metric/Imperial
4 tablespoons oil
225 g/8 oz onions, peeled
  and sliced
2 garlic cloves, peeled and
  crushed
225 g/8 oz courgettes,
  sliced
½ teaspoon mixed dried
  herbs
2 tablespoons chopped
  fresh parsley
salt
freshly ground pepper
1 × 14 oz can tomatoes,
  drained
4 eggs

American
4 tablespoons oil
½ lb onions, peeled and
  sliced
2 garlic cloves, peeled and
  crushed
½ lb zucchini,
  sliced
½ teaspoon mixed dried
  herbs
2 tablespoons chopped
  fresh parsley
salt
freshly ground pepper
1 × 16 oz can tomatoes,
  drained
4 eggs

Heat the oil in a pan, add the onions and garlic and fry for 3 to 4 minutes. Add the courgettes (zucchini) and fry for a further 3 to 4 minutes. Stir in the herbs, parsley, salt, pepper and roughly chopped tomatoes. Put the mixture into an ovenproof dish. Make 4 hollows and break an egg into each. Cook in a preheated moderately hot oven (190°C/375°F, Gas Mark 5) for 10 to 15 minutes or until the eggs are set. Serves 4.

Hidden Eggs

Metric/Imperial	*American*
65 g/2½ oz butter	¼ cup + 1 tablespoon butter
1 tablespoon finely chopped onion	1 tablespoon finely chopped onion
100 g/4 oz mushrooms, chopped	1 cup chopped mushrooms
1 tablespoon chopped fresh parsley	1 tablespoon chopped fresh parsley
salt	salt
freshly ground pepper	freshly ground pepper
½ teaspoon dried basil	½ teaspoon dried basil
4 large tomatoes	4 large tomatoes
4 eggs	4 eggs
4 slices buttered toast	4 slices buttered toast
watercress, to garnish	watercress, to garnish

Use 15 g/½ oz (1 tablespoon) butter to grease a shallow, medium ovenproof dish. Melt 25 g/1 oz (2 tablespoons) of the butter in a frying pan, add the onion and mushrooms and fry until soft. Stir in the parsley, salt, pepper and basil.

Cut a slice from the top of each tomato, carefully scoop out the pulp and put the tomato shells into the prepared dish. Put some mushroom mixture into each tomato and break an egg on top. Sprinkle with salt and pepper and dot each with the remaining butter. Replace the tomato slices and cook in a preheated moderate oven (180°C/350°F, Gas Mark 4) for 8 to 10 minutes or until the eggs are set. Cut rounds of toast slightly larger than the tomatoes and place one under each tomato. Garnish with watercress. Serves 4.

All-In-Egg Breakfast

Metric/Imperial	*American*
1 tablespoon oil	1 tablespoon oil
3 bacon rashers, rind removed, chopped	3 bacon slices, rind removed, chopped
2 slices white bread, crusts removed, cut into cubes	2 slices white bread, crusts removed, cut into cubes
2 tomatoes, cut into wedges	2 tomatoes, cut into wedges
6 eggs	6 eggs
6 teaspoons water	6 teaspoons water
salt	salt
freshly ground pepper	freshly ground pepper

Heat the oil in an omelette or frying pan, add the bacon and cook for a few minutes. Add the bread cubes and cook for a few minutes until crisp and golden brown. Stir in the tomatoes and heat through. Beat together the eggs, water, salt and pepper and pour into the pan. Cook over a low heat until the underside is firm and the top still runny, place the pan under a preheated grill until the top is just set. Cut into 4 wedges. Serves 4.

Eggeree

Metric/Imperial	*American*
50 g/2 oz butter	¼ cup butter
100 g/4 oz long-grain rice, cooked	½ cup long-grain rice, cooked
75 g/3 oz smoked haddock, cooked and flaked	¼ lb finnan haddie or smoked haddock fillets, cooked and flaked
2 eggs	2 eggs
salt	salt
freshly ground pepper	freshly ground pepper

Melt the butter in a large frying pan, add the rice and fish. Mix together and stir until heated through. Beat together the eggs, salt and pepper and stir into the rice mixture. Cook gently over a low heat until the egg sets, stirring occasionally. Serve immediately. Serves 2.

Soufflé Egg and Bacon Toasts

Metric/Imperial	American
4 eggs, separated	4 eggs, separated
4 rashers bacon, cooked and chopped	4 slices bacon, cooked and chopped
4 tablespoons grated cheese	4 tablespoons grated cheese
4 slices buttered toast	4 slices buttered toast
chopped fresh parsley or chives, to garnish	chopped fresh parsley or chives, to garnish

Beat the egg yolks and stir in the bacon and cheese. Whisk the whites until soft peaks form, then fold into the yolk mixture. Divide among the slices of toast, covering the toast completely. Grill under a low heat for 5 minutes and serve immediately, garnished with parsley. Serves 4.

Crowns on Toast

Metric/Imperial	American
2 large eggs, separated	2 large eggs, separated
salt	salt
freshly ground pepper	freshly ground pepper
2 slices wholemeal toast, buttered	2 slices wholemeal toast, buttered

Whisk the egg whites with salt and pepper until soft peaks form. Pile half on to each piece of toast, make a hollow in the centre using a half shell and slip the yolk into the hollow. Bake in a preheated moderate oven (180°C/350°F, Gas Mark 4) until browned and the yolk is set. Serves 2.

Morning Egg Tingler

Metric/Imperial	American
1 egg	1 egg
125 ml/¼ pint orange juice, chilled	⅔ cup orange juice, chilled

Whisk the egg well, then beat into the orange juice. Serve at once. Serves 1.

Dinner Party Dishes

Cold Salmon and Cucumber Soufflé

Cold Salmon and Cucumber Soufflé

Metric/Imperial
1 × 200 g/7 oz can salmon
about 150 ml/¼ pint milk
25 g/1 oz butter
25 g/1 oz plain flour
salt
freshly ground pepper
¼ teaspoon cayenne
3 eggs, separated
15 g/½ oz powdered
   gelatine
3 tablespoons water
75 g/3 oz cucumber,
   peeled and finely
   chopped
finely grated rind and juice
   of ½ lemon
150 ml/¼ pint double
   cream, lightly whipped
To garnish:
cucumber slices
2-3 sprigs watercress
1 tablespoon caviar
   (optional)

American
1 × 7 oz can salmon
about ⅔ cup milk
2 tablespoons butter
¼ cup all-purpose flour
salt
freshly ground pepper
¼ teaspoon cayenne
3 eggs, separated
2 envelopes unflavored
   gelatin
3 tablespoons water
¾ cup peeled and
   chopped cucumber
finely grated rind and juice
   of ½ lemon
⅔ cup heavy cream, lightly
   whipped
To garnish:
cucumber slices
2-3 sprigs watercress
1 tablespoon caviar
   (optional)

Tie a band of foil or greaseproof paper 8 cm/3 inches above the top of a ½ litre/1 pint (½ quart) soufflé dish. Drain the liquor from the salmon and make up to 300 ml/½ pint (1¼ cups) with the milk. Remove the skin and bones and flake the salmon. Melt the butter in a saucepan, add the flour and cook for 1 to 2 minutes. Gradually stir in the milk mixture and simmer for 2 to 3 minutes stirring constantly. Allow to cool.

Add salt, pepper, cayenne and the egg yolks. Dissolve the gelatine in the hot water and stir into the sauce. Add the salmon, cucumber, lemon rind and juice, and the whipped cream. Whisk the egg whites until stiff and fold into the mixture. Pour into the prepared dish and leave until set. Carefully remove the paper or foil and decorate with cucumber, watercress and a little caviar. Serves 4-8.

Eggs with Watercress, page 60; and Oeufs Fruits de Mer, page 61

Eggs with Watercress

Metric/Imperial	*American*
2 bunches of watercress	2 bunches of watercress
5 tablespoons Mayonnaise (page 53)	5 tablespoons Mayonnaise (page 53)
salt	salt
freshly ground pepper	freshly ground pepper
finely grated rind and juice of ½ lemon	finely grated rind and juice of ½ lemon
8 eggs	8 eggs
paprika	paprika
2 tablespoons French dressing	2 tablespoons French dressing
parsley to garnish	parsley to garnish

Remove and discard the tough stalks from the watercress, wash well and put into a saucepan. Cover with cold water, bring to the boil, cover and simmer for 10 minutes. Drain well and chop finely. Mix together the watercress, 3 tablespoons of the mayonnaise, salt, pepper, lemon rind and juice, and spread the mixture over the bottom of a flat serving dish.

Boil the eggs for 5 minutes, shell and arrange them on the watercress mixture. Spoon the remaining mayonnaise over the top of the eggs and sprinkle with paprika. Spoon over the French dressing and sprinkle with parsley. Serve with melba toast as a starter for 8 or use as a buffet dish.

Mushroom and Egg Ramekins

Metric/Imperial	*American*
175 g/6 oz small button mushrooms	1½ cups small mushrooms
1 garlic clove, crushed	1 garlic clove, crushed
150 ml/¼ pint chicken stock	⅔ cup chicken stock
salt	salt
freshly ground pepper	freshly ground black pepper
4 eggs	4 eggs
1 tablespoon chopped fresh parsley	1 tablespoon chopped parsley

Place the mushrooms, garlic and stock in a pan. Simmer uncovered, adding salt and pepper to taste. Meanwhile, poach the eggs and place in 4 ramekin dishes. Stir the parsley into the mushroom mixture, pour over the eggs and serve immediately. Serves 4.

Oeufs Fruits de Mer

Metric/Imperial	American
50 g/2 oz butter	¼ cup butter
40 g/1½ oz plain flour	¼ cup + 2 tablespoons all-purpose flour
450 ml/¾ pint milk	2 cups milk
3 tablespoons single cream	3 tablespoons light cream
3 tablespoons white wine	3 tablespoons white wine
2 egg yolks	2 egg yolks
salt	salt
freshly ground pepper	freshly ground pepper
8 eggs, hard-boiled, shelled and halved	8 eggs, hard-cooked, shelled and halved
1 × 75 g/3 oz can smoked oysters	1 × 3 oz can smoked oysters
1 × 100 g/4 oz jar baby clams, drained	1 × 4 oz jar baby clams, drained
1 × 150 g/5 oz jar mussels, drained	1 × 5 oz jar mussels, drained
2 tablespoons browned breadcrumbs	2 tablespoons browned bread crumbs
fleurons of puff pastry	fleurons of puff pastry

Melt the butter in a saucepan, add the flour and cook for 1 to 2 minutes. Gradually stir in the milk, and simmer for 2 to 3 minutes, stirring. Stir in the cream, wine, egg yolks, salt and pepper. Keep the sauce hot but do not allow to boil. Arrange the egg halves in a shallow flameproof dish and add the oysters, clams and mussels. Pour over the sauce, sprinkle with breadcrumbs and place under a preheated hot grill for 2 to 3 minutes. Garnish with the fleurons, or arrange triangles of toast round the edge. Serve with a green salad. Serves 4.
Variation
In place of the oysters, clams and mussels use canned shrimps and a jar of cockles.

Egg and Mushroom au Gratin

Metric/Imperial	American
100 g/4 oz butter	½ cup butter
225 g/8 oz mushrooms, sliced	2 cups sliced mushrooms
4 eggs	4 eggs
150 ml/¼ pint Hollandaise Sauce (page 51)	⅔ cup Hollandaise Sauce (page 51)
1 tablespoon browned breadcrumbs	1 tablespoon browned bread crumbs
25 g/1 oz cheese, grated	¼ cup grated cheese

Melt the butter in a pan and cook the mushrooms until soft, then turn into a shallow ovenproof dish. Poach the eggs and arrange them on the mushrooms. Pour over the Hollandaise Sauce, sprinkle with the breadcrumbs and cheese. Place under a preheated hot grill for 2 to 3 minutes to heat through and brown the top. Serves 4.

Soufflé Eggs

Metric/Imperial	American
50 g/2 oz butter	¼ cup butter
2 tablespoons browned breadcrumbs	2 tablespoons browned bread crumbs
4 rashers bacon, rind removed, chopped	4 slices bacon, rind removed, chopped
25 g/1 oz plain flour	¼ cup all-purpose flour
150 ml/¼ pint milk	⅔ cup milk
25 g/1 oz cheese, grated	¼ cup grated cheese
salt	salt
freshly ground pepper	freshly ground pepper
¼ teaspoon dry mustard	¼ teaspoon dry mustard
6 eggs	6 eggs

Use 15 g/½ oz (1 tablespoon) of the butter to grease 4 individual 200 ml/⅓ pint (⅞ cup) soufflé dishes, and coat with the breadcrumbs. Put the dishes on a baking sheet. Fry the bacon for 2 to 3 minutes and put in the dishes. Melt the remaining butter in a saucepan, add the flour and cook for 1 to 2 minutes. Gradually stir in the milk and simmer for

Eggs and Mushrooms au Gratin and Soufflé Eggs

2 to 3 minutes, stirring. Add the cheese, salt, pepper and mustard, then allow to cool slightly. Separate 2 of the eggs and add the yolks to the sauce.

Poach the remaining whole eggs until just set, carefully lift out and put one into each soufflé dish. Whisk the egg whites until stiff and fold into the sauce. Spoon some of the mixture over each egg. Cook in a preheated moderately hot oven (190°C/375°F, Gas Mark 5) for 15 to 20 minutes until well risen and firm to the touch. Serve at once with crisp bread rolls. Serves 4.

Eggs in Herb Sauce

Metric/Imperial	American
6-8 eggs	6-8 eggs
1 lettuce	1 head lettuce
Herb Sauce:	*Herb Sauce:*
1 egg yolk	1 egg yolk
150 ml/¼ pint olive oil	⅔ cup olive oil
1½ tablespoons white wine vinegar	1½ tablespoons white wine vinegar
½ tablespoon lemon juice	½ tablespoon lemon juice
150 ml/¼ pint single cream	⅔ cup light cream
40 g/1½ oz chopped fresh mixed herbs: parsley, chives, chervil, dill, tarragon and marjoram	1 cup chopped fresh mixed herbs: parsley, chives, chervil, dill, tarragon and marjoram

Hard-boil the eggs or, if you prefer soft-boiled, boil for exactly 5 minutes, then place in cold water before shelling. Make a mayonnaise with the egg yolk, olive oil, vinegar and lemon juice. Stir in the cream and chopped herbs. These should be so finely chopped that they are almost reduced to a purée.

To serve, make a bed of shredded lettuce leaves on a flat plate and lay the shelled eggs on it. If hard-boiled, they should be cut in half and laid cut side down; if soft-boiled, leave them whole. Pour the green sauce over and serve with buttered wholewheat bread. Serves 6-8.

Oeufs St Germain

Metric/Imperial	American
500 g/1 lb frozen peas, cooked	3 cups frozen peas, cooked
25 g/1 oz butter	2 tablespoons butter
2 tablespoons double cream	2 tablespoons heavy cream
1 tablespoon chopped fresh mint	1 tablespoon chopped fresh mint
4 eggs	4 eggs
4 slices toasted bread, cut into triangles	4 slices toasted bread, cut into triangles

Place the peas, butter, cream and mint in an electric blender and work until smooth. Turn into a pan and heat gently. Meanwhile, boil the eggs for 4 minutes and shell carefully. Spoon the purée into 4 individual serving dishes. Place an egg in each and surround with toast triangles. Serves 4.

Coin Purse Eggs *(Illustrated on page 7)*

Metric/Imperial	American
6-8 tablespoons oil	6-8 tablespoons oil
6 eggs	6 eggs
3 spring onions (shallots), cut into 2.5 cm/1 inch pieces	3 scallions, cut into 1 inch pieces
4 dried Chinese mushrooms, soaked for 20 minutes, drained and quartered	4 dried Chinese mushrooms, soaked for 20 minutes, drained and quartered
100 g/4 oz canned bamboo shoots, drained and cut into 5 mm/¼ inch slices	1 cup canned bamboo shoots, drained and cut into ¼ inch slices
250 ml/8 fl oz clear chicken stock or water	1 cup clear chicken stock or water
2 tablespoons soy sauce	2 tablespoons soy sauce
1 tablespoon dry sherry	1 tablespoon pale dry sherry
2 teaspoons cornflour, dissolved in 2 tablespoons water	2 teaspoons cornstarch, dissolved in 2 tablespoons water

Heat 1 tablespoon of the oil in a pan. Break an egg into it and fry until the edges are set. Turn over carefully and fry the other side until the egg is completely set. Transfer to a serving plate and keep hot. Fry the remaining eggs in the same way, adding more oil to the pan as necessary.

Heat 2 tablespoons of oil in a pan. Add the spring onions (shallots/scallions) and stir-fry until fragrant. Add the mushrooms and bamboo shoots and stir-fry for a few seconds. Stir in the broth or water, soy sauce and sherry and bring to the boil. Add the cornflour (cornstarch) mixture and simmer, stirring, until thickened. Spoon the sauce over the eggs and serve hot. Serves 3-6.

Lunch and Supper Dishes

Eggs on Rice

Metric/Imperial	American
175 g/6 oz long-grain rice	1 cup long-grain rice
4 tablespoons oil	4 tablespoons oil
1 green pepper, cored, seeded and thinly sliced	1 green pepper, cored, seeded and thinly sliced
50 g/2 oz onion, chopped	½ cup chopped onion
175 g/6 oz streaky bacon, rind removed, chopped	9 slices streaky bacon, rind removed, chopped
salt	salt
freshly ground pepper	freshly ground pepper
300 ml/½ pint homemade tomato sauce	1¼ cups homemade tomato sauce
4 poached eggs	4 poached eggs
fresh parsley, to garnish	fresh parsley, to garnish

Boil the rice in salted water for 12 to 15 minutes until cooked. Drain well and keep warm. Meanwhile, heat the oil in a frying pan, add the green pepper and onion and fry for 5 to 6 minutes. Add the bacon and fry for 4 to 5 minutes.

Stir the bacon mixture into the rice, and add salt and pepper to taste. Turn into a shallow dish and spoon some hot sauce down the centre. (Any remaining sauce can be served separately.) Arrange the poached eggs on the sauce and sprinkle with parsley. Serves 4.

Eggs Maryland

Metric/Imperial	American
6 eggs	6 eggs
1 banana	1 banana
2 teaspoons lemon juice	2 teaspoons lemon juice
175 g/6 oz cooked ham, cut into thin strips	¾ cup cooked ham, cut into thin strips
1 × 300 g/11 oz can sweetcorn, drained	1 × 11 oz can kernel corn, drained
salt	salt
freshly ground pepper	freshly ground pepper
150 ml/¼ pint Mayonnaise (page 53)	⅔ cup Mayonnaise (page 53)
watercress, to garnish	watercress, to garnish

Eggs on Rice and Eggs Maryland

Hard-boil 2 of the eggs, shell and cut in half lengthways. Remove the yolks and sieve on to a plate. Cut the whites into thin strips. Peel and thinly slice the banana, and toss in the lemon juice. Mix together the strips of egg whites, ham, sweetcorn, salt, pepper and banana. Put the mixture on to an oval serving dish.

Poach the remaining eggs and arrange them on the mixture. Spoon some mayonnaise over each egg and sprinkle the sieved egg yolk on top. Garnish with watercress. Serves 4.

Egg Pizzas

Metric/Imperial	American
1 small onion, grated	1 small onion, grated
3 tablespoons tomato purée	3 tablespoons tomato paste
1 teaspoon dried oregano	1 teaspoon dried oregano
salt	salt
freshly ground pepper	freshly ground pepper
4 flat bread rolls	4 flat bread rolls
8 hard-boiled eggs	8 hard-cooked eggs
8 black olives	8 ripe olives
225 g/8 oz cheese, grated	2 cups grated cheese
2 eggs, beaten	2 eggs, beaten
½ teaspoon prepared mustard	½ teaspoon prepared mustard
watercress sprigs, to garnish	watercress sprigs, to garnish

Mix together the onion, tomato purée (paste), oregano, salt and pepper. Split the bread rolls and spread the mixture over each half. Cut the hard-boiled eggs in half lengthways and place 2 halves on each half roll, cut side down. Halve the olives and remove the stones then arrange around the eggs. Mix together the grated cheese, beaten eggs and mustard. Spread over the eggs and bake in a preheated hot oven (220°C/425°F, Gas Mark 7) for 10 to 15 minutes until the pizzas are browned. Serve garnished with watercress. Serves 4.

Stuffed Eggs

Metric/Imperial	American
6 large eggs	6 large eggs
3 tablespoons Mayonnaise (page 53) or double cream or 25 g/1 oz soft butter	3 tablespoons Mayonnaise (page 53) or heavy cream or 2 tablespoons soft butter
1 teaspoon French mustard	1 teaspoon Dijon-style mustard
salt	salt
cayenne pepper	cayenne pepper

Boil the eggs in simmering water for 11 minutes, stirring for the first 6 minutes to centre the yolks. Plunge into cold water, lightly cracking the shells. Shell and halve lengthwise with a stainless steel knife (to prevent discoloration). Cut a tiny slice from the bottom of each half to make it flat.

Remove the yolks and put the whites into cold water to prevent drying out. Mix the yolks with mayonnaise, cream or butter, mustard and salt and pepper. Stir in the flavourings (see below). Remove the whites from the water and dry. Pile or pipe the yolk mixture back into the whites. Serve with salad or vegetables as a light meal for 3 or 4.

Variations

Herb Add 1 tablespoon chopped fresh herbs or 1½ tablespoons chopped parsley with ¼ teaspoon dried herbs. Sprinkle with chopped parsley or snipped chives.

Ham and Cheese Add 1 tablespoon finely chopped cooked ham and 2 tablespoons grated Cheddar or blue cheese. Garnish with slivers of ham.

Curry Add 1-2 teaspoons curry powder or curry paste and a spring onion, finely chopped (including some of the green top). Garnish with strips of spring onion.

Eggs in Sweet and Sour Sauce

Metric/Imperial	*American*
4 eggs	4 eggs
oil for frying	oil for frying
Sauce:	*Sauce:*
1 tablespoon cornflour	1 tablespoon cornstarch
4 tablespoons cold water	¼ cup cold water
1 tablespoon soy sauce	1 tablespoon soy sauce
1 tablespoon tomato purée	1 tablespoon tomato paste
1 tablespoon sugar	1 tablespoon sugar
1 tablespoon white wine vinegar	1 tablespoon white wine vinegar
2 tablespoons orange juice	2 tablespoons orange juice

Fry the eggs in oil, arrange on a heated serving dish and keep warm. Mix all the ingredients for the sauce in a small saucepan, bring to the boil and simmer, stirring, until translucent. Pour over the eggs and serve. Serves 4.

Devilled Kidney Scramble

Metric/Imperial	American
1 × 20 cm/8 in short pastry case, baked	1 × 8 in pastry case, baked
50 g/2 oz butter	4 tablespoons butter
1 small onion, chopped	1 small onion, chopped
3 lambs' kidneys, skinned, cored and chopped	3 lambs' kidneys, skinned, cored and chopped
1 tablespoon plain flour	1 tablespoon all-purpose flour
1 teaspoon tomato purée	1 teaspoon tomato paste
few drops Worcestershire sauce	few drops Worcestershire sauce
salt	salt
freshly ground pepper	freshly ground pepper
150 ml/¼ pint chicken stock	¼ cup + 2 tablespoons chicken stock
6 eggs, beaten	6 eggs, beaten

Keep the flan case warm. Melt half the butter in a frying pan and sauté the onion until soft. Add the kidneys and cook for 2 to 3 minutes. Stir in the flour, tomato purée, Worcestershire sauce, salt, pepper and stock. Simmer for 8 to 10 minutes. Melt the remaining butter in a saucepan, add the eggs and cook slowly, stirring constantly until scrambled. Pile into the flan and top with the kidney mixture. Serves 4.

Devilled Kidney Scramble

Spinach Tart

Metric/Imperial	American
175 g/6 oz shortcrust pastry, made with 175 g/6 oz plain flour	1½ cups basic pie dough, made with 1½ cups all-purpose flour
Filling:	Filling:
5 eggs	5 eggs
50 g/2 oz butter	¼ cup butter
225 g/8 oz canned or frozen spinach or 450 g/1 lb fresh spinach, cooked, drained and chopped	½ lb canned or frozen spinach or 1 lb fresh spinach, cooked, drained and chopped
225 g/8 oz cottage cheese	½ lb cottage cheese
salt	salt
freshly ground pepper	freshly ground pepper
¼ teaspoon ground nutmeg	¼ teaspoon ground nutmeg
150 ml/¼ pint single cream	⅔ cup light cream
25 g/1 oz cheese, grated	¼ cup grated cheese

Roll out the pastry and use to line a 20 cm/8 inch flan ring. Line with a piece of foil and cook in a preheated moderately hot oven (200°C/400°F, Gas Mark 6) for 10 minutes. Remove the foil and set the pastry case on one side.

Meanwhile, hard-boil 2 of the eggs, shell and chop them. Melt the butter in a saucepan, add the spinach, well drained if using canned, and heat slowly for 10 to 12 minutes if frozen, 3 to 4 minutes if canned or fresh. Add a little water if necessary but keep as dry as possible. Remove the saucepan from the heat, cool slightly then add the cottage cheese, hard-boiled eggs, a little salt, pepper and the nutmeg, and put into the pastry case. Beat together remaining eggs, cream, salt and pepper and pour over the spinach mixture. Sprinkle over the grated cheese and cook in a preheated moderately hot oven (190°C/375°F, Gas Mark 5) for 25 to 30 minutes. Serve warm with salad. Serves 4-6.

Variation

Spinach and Fish Tart Place 225 g/8 oz flaked, canned or cooked fish in the baked pastry case before adding the spinch. Omit the cottage cheese if liked.

Chakchouka

Metric/Imperial	*American*
2 tablespoons oil	2 tablespoons oil
2 onions, peeled and sliced	2 onions, peeled and sliced
½ teaspoon chilli powder	½ teaspoon chili powder
2 red peppers, cored, seeded and sliced	2 red peppers, cored, seeded and sliced
2 green peppers, cored, seeded and sliced	2 green peppers, cored, seeded and sliced
6 tomatoes, skinned and chopped	6 tomatoes, skinned and chopped
salt	salt
freshly ground pepper	freshly ground pepper
8 eggs	8 eggs

Heat the oil in a frying pan, add the onions and fry until softened. Add the chilli powder and fry for 1 minute, then add the peppers, tomatoes, salt and pepper. Cover and simmer for 10 minutes. Divide the mixture between 4 shallow ovenproof dishes and make 2 hollows in each. Break the eggs into the hollows and season to taste. Place in a preheated moderately hot oven (200°C/400°F, Gas Mark 6) and cook for 7 to 10 minutes, until the eggs are set. Serves 4.

Bean and Egg au Gratin

Metric/Imperial	*American*
500 g/1 oz shelled broad beans	1 lb shelled lima beans
salt	salt
3 hard-boiled eggs, sliced	3 hard-cooked eggs, sliced
50 g/2 oz margarine	¼ cup margarine
40 g/1½ oz wholewheat flour	6 tablespoons wholewheat flour
450 ml/¾ pint milk	2 cups milk
freshly ground pepper	freshly ground pepper
2 tablespoons fresh brown breadcrumbs	2 tablespoons fresh brown bread crumbs
50 g/2 oz Cheddar cheese, grated	½ cup grated Cheddar cheese

Cook the beans in boiling salted water until just tender; drain. Place half the beans in a greased ovenproof dish and place the eggs on top. Cover with the remaining beans.

Melt 40g/1½oz (3 tablespoons) of the margarine in a pan, stir in the flour and cook gently, stirring, to make a roux. Remove from the heat and gradually add the milk, stirring. Return to the heat and bring to the boil. Cook, stirring, until thickened. Season to taste with salt and pepper.

Pour the sauce over the beans and sprinkle on the breadcrumbs and cheese. Dot with the remaining margarine, place in a preheated hot oven (220°C/425°F, Gas Mark 7) and cook for 15 minutes until golden brown. Serve immediately. Serves 4.

Potato Omelette

Metric/Imperial	American
500g/1 lb potatoes, cooked and mashed	2 cups mashed potato
3 eggs, separated	3 eggs, separated
100g/4oz Cheddar cheese, grated	1 cup grated Cheddar cheese
2 tablespoons milk	2 tablespoons milk
1 tablespoon chopped fresh parsley	1 tablespoon chopped fresh parsley
salt	salt
freshly ground pepper	freshly ground pepper
25g/1 oz butter	2 tablespoons butter
To garnish:	To garnish:
cucumber slices	cucumber slices
tomato slices	tomato slices
chopped parsley	chopped parsley

Beat the potato with the egg yolks, cheese, milk, parsley, and salt and pepper to taste. Whisk the egg whites until stiff and fold into the potato mixture. Melt the butter in an omelette pan, add the mixture and cook for 2 minutes on each side. Slide on to a serving plate and cut into quarters. Garnish each portion with cucumber and tomato and sprinkle with chopped parsley. Serve at once with a crisp green salad or vegetables. Serves 4.

Prawn and Egg Curry

Prawn and Egg Curry

Metric/Imperial	American
3 tablespoons oil	3 tablespoons oil
100 g/4 oz onions, sliced	1 cup sliced onions
1 large cooking apple, peeled, cored and chopped	1 large tart apple, peeled, cored and chopped
2-3 tablespoons curry powder	2-3 tablespoons curry powder
1 tablespoon plain flour	1 tablespoon all-purpose flour
1 tablespoon mango chutney	1 tablespoon mango chutney
2 teaspoons tomato purée	2 teaspoons tomato paste
50 g/2 oz sultanas	1/3 cup raisins or golden raisins
1 tablespoon demerara sugar	1 tablespoon brown or raw sugar
1 × 300 g/11 oz can pineapple cubes	1 × 11 oz can pineapple cubes
about 450 ml/3/4 pint light stock or water	2 cups light stock or water
175 ml/6 fl oz soured cream	3/4 cup sour cream
175-225 g/6-8 oz peeled prawns	about 1 cup shelled shrimps
9 eggs, hard-boiled and shelled	9 eggs, hard-cooked and shelled
225 g/8 oz long-grain rice	2 cups long-grain rice

Oriental Eggs, page 76

To serve:	To serve:
desiccated coconut	shredded coconut
mango chutney	mango chutney
sliced banana in lemon	sliced banana in lemon
juice	juice
peanuts	peanuts
poppadoms	poppadoms

Heat the oil in a saucepan, add the onion and fry for 5 to 6 minutes. Add the apple and fry for 2 to 3 minutes. Stir in the curry powder, flour, chutney, tomato purée, sultanas and sugar and cook for 3 to 4 minutes. Drain the juice from the can of pineapple and make up to 600 ml/1 pint (2½ cups) with the stock or water. Stir the liquid into the saucepan, bring to the boil, cover and simmer for 20 to 25 minutes. Add the pineapple, reserving a few pieces, the soured cream, prawns and 8 whole eggs. Heat for a further 5 minutes. Slice the remaining egg.

Cook the rice in boiling salted water for 12 to 15 minutes until just cooked, drain and put into a serving dish. Arrange the whole eggs on top and pour the sauce over. Garnish with the sliced egg and remaining pineapple. Serve with individual dishes of coconut, chutney, banana and peanuts and with poppadoms. Serves 4.

Stuffed Eggs au Gratin

Metric/Imperial
12 stuffed egg halves, any
  flavour (see page 68)
1 × 440 g/15½ oz can
  cream of chicken or
  mushroom soup
4 tablespoons milk
50 g/2 oz butter, melted
2 teaspoons chopped fresh
  chives or parsley
salt
freshly ground pepper
25 g/1 oz fresh
  breadcrumbs, tossed in
  melted butter

American
12 stuffed egg halves, any
  flavor (see page 68)
1 × 15½ oz can of cream of
  chicken or mushroom
  soup
¼ cup milk
¼ cup butter, melted
2 teaspoons chopped fresh
  chives or parsley
salt
freshly ground pepper
½ cup soft bread crumbs,
  tossed in melted butter

Arrange the stuffed eggs in a shallow ovenproof dish. Mix the soup, milk, butter, chives or parsley, salt and pepper and pour over the eggs. Sprinkle with crumbs and bake in a preheated moderate oven (180°C/350°F, Gas Mark 4) for 20 minutes until golden brown and hot. Serves 4 to 6.

Oriental Eggs

Metric/Imperial
8 eggs
2 tablespoons oil
1 carrot, peeled and grated
1 onion, chopped
4 tablespoons clear honey
1 tablespoon soy sauce
salt
freshly ground pepper
2 tablespoons chutney
¼ teaspoon paprika
1 tablespoon cornflour
2 tablespoons cold water
150 ml/¼ pint wine
  vinegar
cooked noodles, to serve

American
8 eggs
2 tablespoons oil
1 carrot, peeled and grated
1 onion, chopped
4 tablespoons honey
1 tablespoon soy sauce
salt
freshly ground pepper
2 tablespoons chutney
¼ teaspoon paprika
1 tablespoon cornstarch
2 tablespoons cold water
¼ cup + 2 tablespoons
  wine vinegar
cooked noodles, to serve

Boil the eggs for 5 minutes, drain, shell, then put them in warm water. Heat the oil in a saucepan, add the carrot and onion and fry for 3 to 4 minutes. Stir in honey, soy sauce, salt, pepper, chutney and paprika. Blend cornflour with the water and stir in the vinegar. Add to the saucepan, bring to the boil, stirring constantly until the mixture thickens. Simmer for 2 to 3 minutes. Drain eggs, prick each with a fork several times then add to the sauce. Heat for a further 2 to 3 minutes. Arrange the hot noodles on a serving dish and pour the eggs and sauce over. Serves 4-8.

Pipérade

Metric/Imperial	*American*
3 tablespoons olive oil	3 tablespoons oil
2 onions, peeled and sliced	2 onions, peeled and sliced
2 green peppers, sliced	2 green peppers, sliced
2 garlic cloves, crushed	2 garlic cloves, crushed
3 large tomatoes, skinned, seeded and chopped	3 large tomatoes, skinned, seeded and chopped
salt	salt
freshly ground pepper	freshly ground pepper
8 eggs	8 eggs
3 tablespoons milk	3 tablespoons milk
15 g/½ oz margarine	1 tablespoon margarine
To garnish:	*To garnish:*
butter	butter
3 small slices wholewheat bread, toasted	3 small slices wholewheat bread, toasted

Heat the oil in a large pan, add the onions and fry until softened. Add the peppers and cook for 5 minutes, then add the garlic, tomatoes and salt and pepper. Simmer until all the ingredients are soft and most of the liquid has evaporated. Beat the eggs and milk together, with salt and pepper to taste. Melt the margarine in a pan, add the eggs and scramble lightly.

Transfer the vegetables to a warmed serving dish, spread the eggs on top and fork a little of the vegetable mixture into the edge of the egg. Surround with small triangles of buttered toast (flavour the butter with garlic if liked). Serve immediately. Serves 6.

Salads

Eggs in Aspic

Metric/Imperial
450 ml/¾ pint liquid aspic
  jelly
4 gherkins
4 eggs, hard-boiled and
  shelled
cress, to garnish

American
2 cups liquid aspic
  jelly
4 gherkins
4 eggs, hard-cooked and
  shelled
cress, to garnish

When the aspic jelly is just beginning to set use some to coat the inside of 4 dariole moulds. Pour 2 teaspoons of jelly in each mould and leave to set. Cut each gherkin in a fan shape, put one in the bottom of each mould and cover with a teaspoon of aspic jelly. Leave to set. Put an egg, rounded end down, into each mould, fill with aspic jelly and leave to set. Put the remaining jelly in a basin and leave to set. Chop the jelly in the basin and arrange on a serving plate. Turn the eggs out and garnish with cress. Serves 4 as a starter or use for a buffet.

Stuffed Egg Salad

Metric/Imperial
1 large carrot, peeled and
  grated
50 g/2 oz cooked beetroot,
  chopped
8 eggs, hard-boiled
2 tablespoons Mayonnaise
  (page 53)
75 g/3 oz full fat soft cheese
salt
freshly ground pepper
cress
paprika

American
1 large carrot, peeled and
  grated
⅓ cup cooked chopped
  beet
8 eggs, hard-cooked
2 tablespoons Mayonnaise
  (page 53)
about ½ cup cream cheese
salt
freshly ground pepper
cress
paprika

Mix together the carrot and beetroot and place in the centre of a round, flat plate. Shell and halve the eggs lengthways. Scoop the yolks out into a basin, add the mayonnaise, cheese, salt and pepper, and beat well together. Pile a spoonful of the mixture on to one-half of egg white and sandwich together with another half. Repeat with the remaining mixture and egg halves. Place the eggs around the salad with cress between each egg. Sprinkle the eggs with paprika. Serve with warm wholemeal rolls and butter as a starter. Serves 8.

Variations

To the egg yolk mixture add one of the following: 2 tablespoons chopped watercress, 50 g/2 oz (⅓ cup) chopped prawns or shrimps, ½ teaspoon tomato purée, ½ teaspoon anchovy essence, ½ teaspoon curry powder or 2 teaspoons capers.

Spiced Egg Salad

Metric/Imperial	American
8 hard-boiled eggs, quartered	8 hard-cooked eggs, quartered
3 green peppers, cored, seeded and chopped	3 green peppers, cored, seeded and chopped
1 red pepper, cored, seeded and sliced	1 red pepper, cored, seeded and sliced
4 mushrooms, sliced	4 mushrooms, sliced
6 black olives	6 pitted ripe olives
1 tablespoon walnuts	1 tablespoon walnuts
Dressing:	*Dressing:*
1 garlic clove, crushed	1 garlic clove, crushed
1 teaspoon paprika pepper	1 teaspoon paprika pepper
2 tablespoons white wine vinegar	2 tablespoons white wine vinegar
6 tablespoons oil	6 tablespoons oil
salt	salt
freshly ground pepper	freshly ground pepper
½ teaspoon sugar	½ teaspoon sugar

Arrange the eggs, green and red peppers, mushrooms and olives in a salad bowl. Sprinkle over the walnuts. In a screw-top jar combine all the dressing ingredients. Shake well and pour the dressing over the salad. Chill for 30 minutes before serving. Serves 4.

Devilled Cottage Eggs

Metric/Imperial	American
4 hard-boiled eggs	4 hard-cooked eggs
¼ teaspoon dry mustard	¼ teaspoon dry mustard
2 teaspoons vinegar	2 teaspoons vinegar
1 tablespoon chutney	1 tablespoon chutney
225 g/8 oz cottage cheese	1 cup cottage cheese
¼ teaspoon salt	¼ teaspoon salt
pinch of paprika	pinch of paprika
1 teaspoon chopped fresh chives	1 teaspoon chopped fresh chives
shredded lettuce	shredded lettuce
parsley sprigs	parsley sprigs

Cut the eggs in half lengthwise and remove the yolks. Mash with the mustard, vinegar and chutney. Add the cheese and mix well. Add salt and paprika to taste. Stir in the chives. Fill the egg whites with the mixture. Arrange on a bed of shredded lettuce and garnish with parsley sprigs. Serves 4.

Egg Pasta, and Fish Salad

This salad may be made with any shape of pasta – noodles, spaghetti, shells, etc.

Metric/Imperial	American
225 g/8 oz spinach pasta	½ lb spinach pasta
salt	salt
4 hard-boiled eggs cut in wedges	4 hard-cooked eggs cut in wedges
100 g/4 oz cooked shelled mussels	½ cup cooked shelled mussels or clams
100 g/4 oz peeled prawns, cooked	½ cup shelled shrimp, cooked
1 × 50 g/2 oz can anchovies, drained	1 × 2 oz can anchovies, drained
50 g/2 oz button mushrooms, sliced	½ cup sliced button mushrooms
2 tomatoes, cut into wedges	2 tomatoes, cut into wedges
150 ml/¼ pint dressing (see Spiced Egg Salad page 80)	⅔ cup dressing (see Spiced Egg Salad page 80)
To garnish:	To garnish:
2 tablespoons chopped parsley	2 tablespoons chopped parsley
2 tablespoons grated Parmesan cheese	2 tablespoons grated Parmesan cheese

Cook the pasta in plenty of boiling salted water for 10 to 15 minutes until 'al dente'. Drain in a colander and rinse under cold running water. Drain thoroughly.

Put the cooked pasta in a bowl, then add the eggs, fish, mushrooms and tomatoes. Pour on the dressing and mix gently. Sprinkle with parsley and Parmesan. Serves 4.

Desserts

Crêpes Suzette

Metric/Imperial
100 g/4 oz unsalted butter
finely grated rind and juice
  of 1 orange
100 g/4 oz caster sugar
8 thin pancakes (see basic
  recipe page 39)
2 tablespoons Orange
  Curaçao, Cointreau or
  Grand Marnier
2 tablespoons brandy

American
½ cup unsalted butter
finely grated rind and juice
  of 1 orange
½ cup sugar
8 thin pancakes (see basic
  recipe page 39)
2 tablespoons Orange
  Curaçao, Cointreau or
  Grand Marnier
2 tablespoons brandy

Cream the butter with the orange rind. Add the sugar, a tablespoon at a time, pouring a little orange juice on the butter, and beat both in together to prevent the liquid separating from the fat. Heat the flavoured butter gently in a frying pan and put the pancakes in one at a time, spooning the sauce over them. Fold each pancake in half and then in half again, push to the side of the pan and put in the next one.

When all the pancakes are folded and the sauce slightly thickened, pour over the orange liqueur. Warm the brandy in a ladle or small pan, ignite it, and pour over the pancakes. Serve immediately. Serves 4.

Soufflé Omelette Grand Marnier

Metric/Imperial
2 eggs, separated
2 teaspoons water
4 teaspoons caster sugar
15 g/½ oz butter
125 g/4 oz fresh fruit,
  peeled and sliced
2 tablespoons Grand
  Marnier, warmed

American
2 eggs, separated
2 teaspoons water
4 teaspoons sugar
1 tablespoon butter
1 cup peeled and sliced
  fresh fruit
2 tablespoons Grand
  Marnier, warmed

Beat together egg yolks, water and half the sugar until creamy and light in colour. Whisk egg whites until stiff and fold into yolk mixture. Melt the butter in an 18-20 cm/7-

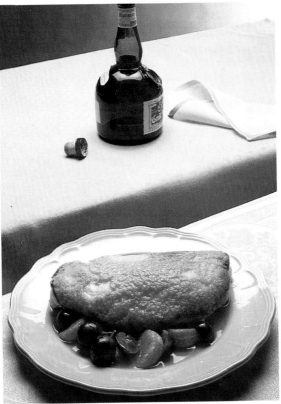

Soufflé Omelette Grand Marnier

8 inch omelette pan, pour in the mixture and cook over a low heat until most of the egg mixture has set and the underneath is golden. Put under a pre-heated grill for 1 to 2 minutes to set the top of the omelette. Make a slit across the centre of the omelette, place the fruit close to the slit and fold the omelette in half away from the pan's handle. Tilt the pan over so the omelette falls out on to a flameproof plate. Sprinkle with remaining sugar, pour over the Grand Marnier and ignite. Serves 1-2.

Variation

Sprinkle omelette with icing sugar and score with two metal skewers heated over a flame until red hot.

Coffee Praline Soufflé

Metric/Imperial	American
50 g/2 oz caster sugar	¼ cup sugar
50 g/2 oz unblanched almonds	½ cup unblanched almonds
Soufflé:	*Soufflé:*
3 eggs, separated	3 eggs, separated
75 g/3 oz sugar	6 tablespoons sugar
2 tablespoons instant coffee granules	2 tablespoons instant coffee granules
175 ml/6 fl oz boiling water	¾ cup boiling water
12 g/½ oz (envelope) powdered gelatine	2 envelopes unflavored gelatin
3 tablespoons cold water	3 tablespoons cold water
300 ml/½ pint double cream	1¾ cups heavy cream
2 tablespoons Tia Maria	2 tablespoons Tia Maria

Prepare a 15 cm/6 inch soufflé dish. To make the praline, put the sugar and almonds into a small thick saucepan over gentle heat. When the sugar is dissolved, stir carefully to coat the almonds and continue cooking until rich golden brown and smelling of toffee. Pour on to an oiled baking tin, spreading it out. When cold and brittle, remove and chop small or grind in a mill, but not to fine powder.

Mix the egg yolks and sugar in a large bowl. Dissolve the coffee in the boiling water and add gradually. Whisk over a saucepan of boiling water until thick and foamy. Remove from the heat and continue whisking until cold. Soak the gelatine in the cold water, dissolve over gentle heat and stir into the soufflé mixture. Place in a basin of cold water with ice and stir gently from time to time until beginning to set.

Meanwhile whisk the egg whites until stiff but not dry. Whip cream into soft peaks and fold about two-thirds into the coffee mixture. Fold in the egg whites and half the praline. Mix in the Tia Maria. Turn into the soufflé dish, smooth the top and chill. When set, peel off paper collar with the help of a knife dipped in hot water. Coat the sides of the soufflé with some of the remaining praline. Whip remaining cream stiff enough to pipe and decorate the soufflé. Decorate with the rest of the praline. Serves 4.

Clafoutis Limousin

Metric/Imperial	*American*
75 g/3 oz plain flour	¾ cup all-purpose flour
pinch of salt	pinch of salt
3 tablespoons caster sugar	3 tablespoons sugar
2 eggs, beaten	2 eggs, beaten
300 ml/½ pint milk	1½ cups milk
1 tablespoon Kirsch or rum	1 tablespoon Kirsch or rum
40 g/1½ oz butter, melted	3 tablespoons butter, melted
500 g/1 lb ripe cherries	1 lb ripe cherries

Sift the flour and salt into a mixing bowl and stir in 2 tablespoons of sugar. Add the eggs, and gradually beat in the milk and Kirsh or rum. Cover and leave for 30 minutes. Grease a shallow 1.2 litre/2 pint (5 cup) baking dish with some butter. Whisk the remaining butter into the batter. Put the cherries into the dish and pour over the batter. Bake in a preheated hot oven (220°C/425°F, Gas Mark 7) for 30 minutes, or until golden brown and set. Sprinkle with the remaining sugar and serve. Serves 4-6.

Apricot Amber

Metric/Imperial	*American*
300 ml/½ pint sweetened apricot purée, warm	1¼ cups sweetened apricot purée, warm
lemon juice to taste	lemon juice to taste
25 g/1 oz butter	2 tablespoons butter
2 eggs, separated	2 eggs, separated
50 g/2 oz caster sugar	¼ cup sugar

Sharpen the purée to taste with lemon juice. Stir in the butter and beaten egg yolks. Pour the mixture into a greased shallow pie dish. Whisk the egg whites to a stiff snow and fold in the sugar. Cover the fruit mixture completely with the meringue and ruffle the top. Dredge with sugar. Bake in the centre of a preheated moderate oven (160°C/325°F, Gas Mark 3) for 30 to 35 minutes or until the meringue is crisp and golden. Serve hot or cold. Serves 4.

Cranberry Pancakes

Cranberry Pancakes

Metric/Imperial	*American*
100 g/4 oz plain flour	1 cup all-purpose flour
pinch of salt	pinch of salt
2 eggs	2 eggs
300 ml/½ pint milk	1¼ cups milk
butter for frying	butter for frying
1 × 375 g/13 oz jar whole cranberry sauce	1 × 13 oz jar jellied cranberry sauce
Topping:	*Topping:*
150 ml/¼ pint soured cream	⅔ cup sour cream
2 tablespoons demerara sugar	2 tablespoons brown or raw sugar
25 g/1 oz flaked almonds, toasted	¼ cup sliced or slivered almonds
½ teaspoon ground cinnamon	½ teaspoon ground cinnamon
2 tablespoons sherry	2 tablespoons sherry

Sift together the flour and salt into a basin. Add the eggs and gradually beat in the milk. In a 13-15 cm/5-6 inch frying pan, melt a little butter and use the batter to make 8 to 12 pancakes. Divide the cranberry sauce between the pancakes, roll up and put into a shallow flameproof dish. Keep warm.

To make the topping, mix together the soured cream, half of the sugar, almonds, cinnamon and sherry. Pour over the pancakes and sprinkle on the remaining sugar. Put the dish under a preheated hot grill for several minutes until golden brown. Serves 4.

Orange Caramel Cream

Metric/Imperial	American
Caramel:	*Caramel:*
100 g/4 oz caster sugar	½ lb cup sugar
3 tablespoons water	3 tablespoons water
Orange Custard:	*Orange Custard:*
finely grated rind of	finely grated rind of
1 orange	1 orange
300 ml/½ pint fresh or	1¼ cups fresh or frozen
frozen orange juice	orange juice
3 eggs	3 eggs
40 g/1½ oz sugar	3 tablespoons sugar

Infuse the orange rind in the juice over very gentle heat. Warm 4 × 100 ml/4 oz (½ cup) dariole moulds in the oven so that the caramel does not set too quickly. Put the sugar and water into a thick saucepan and stir over gentle heat until dissolved into clear syrup. Boil briskly, without stirring, until rich caramel colour. Divide between moulds, and wearing thick oven gloves to prevent burning, revolve moulds so that each is evenly coated. Work quickly before caramel hardens.

Beat the eggs and sugar together until light and fluffy. Strain in hot orange juice, mixing well. Pour into prepared moulds and put them in a baking tin with 2.5 cm/1 inch of water. Cover with greased paper and cook in a preheated moderate oven (180°C/350°F, Gas Mark 4) for 1 hour until set and firm. Chill thoroughly. Unmould into individual dishes. Serves 4.

Queen of Puddings

Metric/Imperial	American
75 g/3 oz fresh white breadcrumbs	1½ cups fresh white bread crumbs
25 g/1 oz sugar	2 tablespoons sugar
2 teaspoons grated lemon peel	2 teaspoons grated lemon peel
25 g/1 oz butter	2 tablespoons butter
450 ml/¾ pint milk	2 cups milk
2 eggs, separated	2 eggs, separated
2 tablespoons jam	2 tablespoons jam
50 g/2 oz caster sugar	¼ cup sugar

Mix together the breadcrumbs and sugar. Place the lemon peel, butter and milk in a saucepan and heat gently until the butter melts. Pour over the breadcrumbs and leave to soak for 30 minutes. Beat egg yolks and blend into the cool mixture. Pour into a well greased 900 ml/1½ pint (3¾ cup) ovenproof dish. Bake in a preheated warm oven (160°C/325°F, Gas Mark 3) for 30 minutes or until firm.

Warm the jam and spread over the pudding. Whisk the egg whites until stiff and fold in the sugar using a metal spoon. Pile meringue mixture on top of the pudding and dredge with a little extra sugar if liked. Return the pudding to the oven and bake for 30 minutes or until topping is crisp and golden. Serves 4.

Chocolate Roulade

Metric/Imperial	American
6 eggs, separated	6 eggs, separated
¼ teaspoon vanilla essence	¼ teaspoon vanilla
250 g/8 oz sugar	1 cup sugar
50 g/2 oz cocoa	½ cup cocoa
Filling:	Filling:
300 ml/½ pint whipping cream	1¼ cups thick cream
1 tablespoon sugar	1 tablespoon sugar
a few drops vanilla essence or brandy to taste	a few drops vanilla or brandy to taste

Line a 33×21 cm/13×8½ in Swiss roll tin with greaseproof paper. Whisk egg yolks, vanilla essence and sugar until creamy. Fold in sifted cocoa. Whisk egg whites until stiff and carefully fold into mixture. Pour into prepared tin and spread mixture evenly into the corners. Bake in a pre-heated moderate oven (180°C/350°F, Gas Mark 4) for 20 minutes or until springy to the touch. Remove from oven and turn out on to a sugared piece of greaseproof paper. Roll up Swiss roll style and leave to cool.

Whisk cream with sugar and vanilla or brandy until thick. Unroll the roulade and spread with cream. Carefully re-roll. Transfer to a serving dish and decorate with a little extra cream and a scattering of caster sugar. Serves 8.

Crème Brûlée

Metric/Imperial	American
600 ml/1 pint double cream	2½ cups heavy cream
½ teaspoon vanilla essence	½ teaspoon vanilla
6 egg yolks	6 egg yolks
25 g/1 oz caster sugar	2 tablespoons sugar
50 g/2 oz soft brown or caster sugar, to serve	⅓ cup light brown sugar or sugar, to serve

Put the cream and vanilla into a saucepan and heat gently to scalding point, when bubbles will appear round the edge of the pan. In a basin beat together the egg yolks and caster sugar until pale in colour. Gradually beat in the cream and pour into individual ramekin dishes. Stand the dishes in a baking tin with warm water to come halfway up the dishes. Cook in a preheated moderate oven (160°C/325°F, Gas Mark 3) for 20 to 25 minutes. Remove the dishes from the tin and leave until cold, preferably overnight in the refrigerator. Sprinkle the soft brown sugar or caster sugar over the custards, place under a preheated low grill until the sugar has melted and caramelized. Chill for 2 to 3 hours before serving. Serve with fresh fruit, such as raspberries. Serves 4-6.

Variation
Arrange fresh, poached or canned fruit in the dishes before pouring the custard mixture.

Separate Story

Here is a selection of recipes that make use of either egg whites or yolks. Use them next time you find yourself with an excess of whites or yolks.

Egg Whites

○ Use egg whites to make water ices and sorbets – **Lemon water ice** Dissolve 225 g/8 oz (1 cup) caster sugar in 600 ml/1 pint (2½ cups) water over a low heat. Add the thinly pared rind of 3 lemons and boil gently for 10 minutes; leave to cool. Add the juice of 3 lemons and strain the mixture into a suitable container and place in a freezer or freezing compartment of a refrigerator and freeze until a mushy consistency. Turn the mixture into a bowl and fold in 1 whisked egg white. Return to the container and re-freeze.

○ Whisk 1 egg white into 300 ml/½ pint (1¼ cups) whipped cream to lighten and increase the quantity.

○ Add whisked egg whites to fruit purées to make delicious fools and snows.

○ Give fruits such as grapes or cherries, or the rims of glasses, an attractive frosting by dipping them in lightly beaten egg white, then in caster sugar.

○ Make a meringue topping that can be used for a variety of fruit desserts. Gradually whisk 50 g/2 oz (¼ cup) caster sugar into each stiffly whisked egg white. Pile on to cooked fruit and bake in a preheated moderate oven (180°C/350°F, Gas Mark 4) for about 10 minutes.

○ Make meringues (see page 44) and store in an airtight container for future use.

Coffee Meringue Bombe

Metric/Imperial	American
15 g/½ oz butter	1 tablespoon butter
25 g/1 oz caster sugar	2 tablespoons sugar
Meringue:	*Meringue:*
4 egg whites	4 egg whites
50 g/2 oz granulated sugar	¼ cup sugar
1 tablespoon instant coffee powder	1 tablespoon instant coffee powder
175 g/6 oz caster sugar	¾ cup sugar

Coffee Meringue Bombe

Topping:
300 ml/½ pint double or
  whipping cream
1 × 300 g/11 oz can
  mandarin oranges, well
  drained, or thinly sliced
  fresh oranges
chocolate dessert topping

Topping:
1¼ cups heavy
  cream
1 × 11 oz can mandarin
  oranges, well drained, or
  thinly sliced fresh
  oranges
chocolate dessert topping

Use the butter to grease a 1 litre/2 pint (5 cup) heatproof mixing bowl and coat the inside with the caster sugar. Place the basin in a roasting tin with warm water about 5 cm/2 inches up the basin. Whisk the egg whites until stiff. Mix together the granulated sugar and coffee and gradually whisk into the egg whites. Fold in the caster sugar and pour the mixture into the prepared basin. Cook on a low shelf in a preheated moderate oven (180°C/350°F, Gas Mark 5) for 45 to 60 minutes, until well risen above the basin and firm to the touch. Remove the basin from the water and leave for 10 minutes, then turn the basin upside down on to a serving plate. Remove the basin when cool. Whip the cream until thick and use to cover the meringue. Decorate with orange and dribble over the chocolate sauce. Serves 6-8.

Basic Pavlova

Metric/Imperial	American
6 egg whites	6 egg whites
pinch of salt	pinch of salt
450 g/1 lb caster sugar	2 cups sugar
1½ teaspoons vinegar	1½ teaspoons vinegar
1½ teaspoons	1½ teaspoons
vanilla essence	vanilla
fruit filling (see below)	fruit filling (see below)

If you have a gas oven, preheat it to hot (230°C/450°F, Gas Mark 8) before starting to mix the pavlova. Just before you put the pavlova in the oven, reduce the temperature to cool (150°C/300°F, Gas Mark 2). If you have an electric oven, preheat the oven to cool from the beginning.

Beat the egg whites with salt until soft peaks form, then add the sugar, a tablespoon at a time, beating well between each addition. Lightly fold in the vinegar and vanilla. Draw a circle 18 cm/7 inches in diameter on greaseproof (parchment) paper or foil and place on a baking sheet. Brush the paper with oil. Heap the pavlova mixture into the circle and use the back of a spoon to make a slight depression in the centre. Bake for 40 to 50 minutes, until crisp on top and pale straw colour. Turn off the heat and leave in the oven until cold. Peel off the paper and fill with cream and fruit (see below). Serves 8.

Fillings

Fill the Pavlova generously with whipped cream and then with your choice of fruit. Passionfruit and strawberries, kiwi fruit, fresh or canned peaches, plums or apricots, or sliced banana dipped in lemon juice and sprinkled with toasted coconut are all delicious. Drain canned fruits well.

Seven-Minute Frosting

Metric/Imperial	American
1 egg white	1 egg white
175 g/6 oz caster sugar	¾ cup sugar
pinch of salt	pinch of salt
2 tablespoons water	2 tablespoons water
pinch of cream of tartar	pinch of cream of tartar

Place all the ingredients in a heatproof basin and whisk lightly. Place the bowl over a saucepan of hot water over low heat and continue whisking until the mixture thickens and forms peaks – about 7 minutes. Remove from the heat and continue whisking for a further 2 minutes before using to coat an 18 cm/7 inch cake.

Egg Yolks

○ Make mayonnaise (see page 53). It keeps well if refrigerated. Alternatively enhance your next dinner party with an egg-based sauce (see page 50).

○ Use spare egg yolks to enrich soups and sauces; add to the liquid slowly and avoid high temperatures, which will cause curdling.

○ Sauce Suprême: Stir 1 to 2 egg yolks and 2 to 3 tablespoons single cream into 300 ml/½ pint (1¼ cups) Velouté sauce and use as a basis for fricassées.

○ Add beaten egg yolks to mashed potatoes for extra flavour, or for special occasions pipe into rosettes to make duchesse potatoes.

○ For a healthy morning drink, beat an egg yolk into a glass of chilled orange juice with 1 teaspoon honey.

○ As a quick snack use egg yolks to make tasty Welsh Rarebit: Place 225 g/8 oz (2 cups) grated Cheddar cheese, 150 ml/¼ pint (⅔ cup) brown ale, 2 egg yolks, 40 g/1½ oz (3 tablespoons) butter, ¼ teaspoon salt, ¼ teaspoon freshly ground black pepper and a dash of Worcestershire sauce into a saucepan and heat gently, stirring occasionally until smooth and creamy. Pile the mixture on to 4 slices of hot toast and serve immediately.

○ Children will love this rich mouth-watering cake icing and filling. Beat 2 egg yolks in a deep bowl. Place 75 g/3 oz (6 tablespoons) sugar and 4 tablespoons water in a pan and heat to dissolve the sugar without boiling. Bring to the boil and boil rapidly for 2 to 3 minutes until the temperature reaches 107°C/225°F on a sugar thermometer. Pour the syrup over the egg yolks and whisk constantly until the mixture is thick, cold and mousse-like. Whisk 175 g/6 oz (¾ cup) butter until pale and fluffy and then gradually beat in the egg syrup. Flavour with coffee essence, melted chocolate, lemon or orange zest.

Cold Zabaglione

Metric/Imperial	*American*
150 ml/¼ pint water	⅔ cup water
100 g/4 oz granulated sugar	½ cup sugar
4 egg yolks	4 egg yolks
2 tablespoons sherry or Marsala	2 tablespoons sherry or Marsala
150 ml/¼ pint double or whipping cream	⅔ cup heavy cream
To decorate:	*To decorate:*
1 teaspoon finely grated orange rind	1 teaspoon finely grated orange rind
1 tablespoon chopped nuts	1 tablespoon chopped nuts

Put the water and sugar into a saucepan and heat until the sugar has dissolved, then boil for 3 to 4 minutes until a drop forms a soft ball in a cup of cold water, or it reaches 115°C/239°F on a cooking thermometer.

Put the egg yolks into a basin and gradually whisk in the syrup. Stir in the sherry. Whisk the cream until thick and fold into the mixture. Pour into glasses and leave to set. Mix together the orange rind and nuts and sprinkle on top before serving. Serves 4.

Index

Cold Zabaglione; Individual Almond Soufflés, page 36

All photography by Robert Golden except the following:
Melvin Grey 7, Roger Phillips 2/3.
Illustrations: Oriel Harris